THE WORLD OF THE SWAN

LIVING WORLD BOOKS

John K. Terres, Editor

The World of the
Swan

With Text and Photographs by

Joe Van Wormer

J. B. Lippincott Company
Philadelphia and New York

U.S. Library of Congress Cataloging in Publication Data

Van Wormer, Joe.
  The world of the swan.

  (Living world books)
  SUMMARY: Describes the physical characteristics, habits, and life cycle
of seven species of swans.
  Bibliography: p.
  1. Swans.   [1. Swans]   I. Title.
QL696.A5V35   598.4'1   77–39150
ISBN–0–397–00845–7
ISBN–0–397–00869–4 (lib. bdg.)

To my grandson
Neal Joseph Skorpen

Contents

The World of the Swan

Trumpeter swans.

Meet the Swan

EARLY ONE SPRING MORNING, many years ago, near the Hart Mountain National Antelope Refuge in south-central Oregon, I crawled through frost-tinged sagebrush to a point where I could look out over Flagstaff Lake. Around its northern perimeter in a mile-long crescent of brilliant white, several thousand whistling swans were resting, making a stopover on their migration to nesting grounds in the Arctic wilderness of Alaska.

A contented babble of swan conversation filled this high desert basin. Most of the birds were feeding, or preening, or just sitting. There were some, possibly more restless than the others, constantly taking off in pairs or in small groups to fly up and down the shoreline.

This was my first look at wild swans, and to see them in such numbers was overwhelming. I remember thinking that I had not realized there were that many swans in the world. I spent most of the day hidden in the brush watching them and studying their flight. Occasionally, a circling group would fly overhead, some no more than a hundred feet above the earth. I could hear the soft whisper of their wings and their constant calls. These splendid birds, sharply etched against the cloudless blue sky, moved with deceptive swiftness on the measured beat of wings that spread over 6 feet.

The fact that the birds flew so easily and gracefully came as a surprise because I had never seen a swan fly before. Like most peo-

13

Whistling swans make a rest stop in eastern Oregon.

ple's, all my previous experience with swans had been in public parks where beautiful big white birds swam around majestically, intimidating the other park waterfowl and accepting handouts of bread scraps from park visitors. This was a "swan"—a large all-white bird with a long neck often beautifully arched, as if the bird were consciously posing to look its best. Most park visitors, I am sure, think of these park swans as nonflying birds. Few realize that in their natural state all swans fly, and that those in parks have usually been wing-clipped or pinioned so that they cannot fly.

Furthermore, the swan with which most of us are acquainted, which typifies "swans," is the mute swan, imported many years ago into the United States from Europe. At an early age children become acquainted with this magnificent bird through pictures and prose that generally depict the swan as the epitome of grace, beauty and elegance.

The mute swan is typical of swans and has all the swan attributes,

14

but it is only one of seven species in the world. According to Winston E. Banko in his book about the North American trumpeter swan, classification by the American Ornithologists' Union places swans in the order Anseriformes, the family Anatidae and in three genera—*Olor, Cygnus* and *Chenopis*—of which there are seven species: *

Olor cygnus	Whooper swan
Olor bewicki	Bewick's swan
Olor columbianus	Whistling swan
Olor buccinator	Trumpeter swan
Cygnus olor	Mute swan
Cygnus melancoriphus	Black-necked swan
Chenopis atratus	Black swan

Although these various species are known from widely separated places in the world—northern North America, Europe and Asia, Australia and southern South America—they have much in common.

Swans are all large majestic birds, some weighing up to 30 or even 40 pounds, with a 6- to 8-foot wingspread. Their extremely long necks are as long as, or longer than, the body. All are white except the black swan of Australia and the black-necked swan of South America. Their short strong legs grow farther back than in geese. This makes them awkward and clumsy on land, but in water they swim with stately grace. They are well adapted to a specialized life in shallow water, where they eat large amounts of leafy water plants and with the head and neck submerged dig and root out succulent roots and tubers that grow in pond, lake or stream bottoms.

Editor's Note: Of these, only four species—the mute swan, whooper swan, whistling swan and trumpeter swan—are known in North America, and only the whistling swan and trumpeter swan are natives. The mute swan has been introduced; the whooper swan is an occasional visitor in Greenland, and "accidental" on St. Paul Island and Amchitka in Alaska, and in Maine.

Swans' feet are relatively larger than those of geese and have four toes. The hind toe is small, slightly elevated and free. Three toes protrude forward and are joined by two fully developed webs.

The space between the eye and the bill is called the lore. It is bare in adults but covered with feathers in the very young as well as in some immature birds. The bill, high at the base, is broad and flattened at the tip, which has a somewhat flat horny nail. The bill is covered with a thin leathery skin and has some form of horny toothing or stiff fringe along the edge. These toothlike serrations (the lamellae) along the edges of both mandibles fit together to form a strainer that permits the bird to extract food particles from water taken into the mouth.

A male mute swan in its typical pose. The stains on the head and neck are from minerals in the water.

Males and females resemble each other in appearance and have voices that are much the same, although the female's is slightly higher in pitch. They apparently mate for life, but if one of a pair is lost, it is believed that the other will eventually seek another mate. Only rarely does a male exchange his female for another or become a polygamist.

Although adult wild swans, while nesting or with young, are usually seen only in pairs, Winston E. Banko noted three adult trumpeter swans together one summer south of the Red Rock Lakes National Wildlife Refuge and three other adults accompanied by three cygnets on Icehouse Creek Reservoir. These three adults returned to the reservoir the following year, and one female nested successfully. Obviously, a male and female were in the group of three adults in which

The feet of a trumpeter swan.

The head of a trumpeter swan, showing the bill.

the female nested and raised young, but the sex of the odd bird was not determined.

Mute swans that have lived mostly under domesticated or semi-domesticated conditions for hundreds of years show a stronger tendency to change mates than do the wild species. Also, nonbreeding pairs show a higher percentage of separations than breeding pairs, indicating that the pair bonds of nonbreeding pairs are not so strong as those of breeding pairs. Some rather unusual pairings and separations have been reported. The male of a pair that had nested successfully through two breeding seasons lost his mate to another male. After one year of bachelorhood, he re-paired with his original mate.

One female was reported to have a remarkable record; over a period of six years she occupied three territories and had four mates.

Swans molt only once each year; all the flight feathers are shed simultaneously and the birds become flightless for a while.

Males are called "cobs," females "pens" and the young "cygnets."

Mute Swan (*Cygnus olor*). Some consider the mute swan the handsomest of all swans because of its posturings, proportions and general conduct. Both sexes have all-white plumage and a rather long pointed tail. The eyes are brown surrounded by a narrow bluish-gray ring. Some show brown coloring on their heads and neck—the result of feeding in mud or water that contains iron compounds. It is a stain rather than a natural feather color and is evident in all white swan species. The

The black forehead knob on the mute swan is unique to this species.

upper mandible of the mute swan is pinkish orange with some black on the borders, around the nostrils and on the nail. The lower mandible is blackish at the base but flesh colored toward the tip. On the forehead at the base of the bill there is a prominent black knob. The mute is the only all-white swan that has such a knob.

The mute swan usually carries its long neck in a graceful *S*-shaped curve with the bill inclined downward. Our native swans, the whistler and the trumpeter, typically hold the neck straight, keeping the head erect and the bill horizontal. Although not quite so big as the trumpeter swan, the mute is a large bird with a wingspread exceeding 7 feet.

In England and France the mute swan is colloquially called a wild swan (*cygne sauvage*). The name "mute" is misleading. Though not

A female mute swan settles down on her eggs.

so noisy as other species it hisses when angry; it snorts explosively when excited; when calling its young it utters a noise similar to the bark of a small dog; it even emits an occasional loud trumpetlike sound.

There is a color phase of the mute called the Polish swan in a restricted area along the coast of the Baltic Sea (within the region once known as East Prussia and Poland). Ornithologists disagree as to how this bird should be classified. Some apparently consider it a localized domesticated variation of the mute swan, whereas others want to classify it separately as *Cygnus immutabilis,* the "immutable swan." The adult "immutable" is described as being slightly smaller than the mute, with a clear yellow bill. Legs and feet have been variously described as rosy pink and fleshy gray. In this species cygnets are born white, not gray like the young of other swan species.

In the wild, the mute swan breeds in the British Isles, Denmark, southern Scandinavia, northern Germany, Poland, eastern, central and southern Russia and the lower Danube Valley. It is also native to Asia Minor, Iran, Turkestan, Mongolia, eastern Siberia and Ussuriland.

Although its migrations are not so extensive as those of other wild swans of Europe and Asia, it does leave the colder parts of its breeding range and move southward to spend the winter in southern Europe, northern Africa and southwestern Asia. It has also been known to migrate to northwestern India and Korea, and it appears casually in Japan. Because of their beauty, mute swans have been introduced into ponds, lakes and rivers throughout most of the world, creating a large sedentary domesticated population.

Feral mute swans are quite common in England. One recent estimate puts the population at about 19,000 in Great Britain. The world population of these birds is not known, but there seems to be no existing danger to it.

Although mute swans were imported into North America as "pond swans" on lakes of private estates along the lower Hudson River and on Long Island, N.Y., small feral populations have developed. Wild mute swans now range to eastern Massachusetts, Rhode Island, New Jersey, Ohio, Pennsylvania, West Virginia, Michigan and possibly in other areas that have not yet been publicized.

One such feral population exists in central Oregon in and around the town of Bend. Here the Deschutes River flows through the center

The trumpeter swan.

of town and is dammed in several places to form three small ponds that follow one another like stairsteps. The first is used as a millpond by a large pine mill; the second supports a small electric power plant; the third provides water for ranch irrigation. Each pond has its resident pair of mute swans; the male (and sometimes the female) is pinioned. Despite the numerous hazards to their existence, these adult birds raise many cygnets. As the young birds reach maturity, the older males, jealous of their mates and territories, harass the young males until finally they take to the air and move to nearby bodies of water. Young females generally follow when it comes time for them to pair up. On one lake 6 miles away from Bend and covering roughly a half square mile in area a dozen of these feral mute swans were seen at one time.

Trumpeter Swan (*Olor buccinator*). The trumpeter is the largest of all swans. It weighs 30 pounds on the average, but some individuals may be as heavy as 40 pounds. It has a total length of around 5 feet and a wingspread of from 6 feet to 8 feet 2 inches, according to Banko. Both sexes are pure white except for occasional rusty stains on the head and neck. The eyes are brown. The long bill is black except for a narrow red border to the upper mandible which makes the bird appear to be wearing a slight grin. (Unfortunately, this red border is not exclusively a trumpeter swan trademark and therefore is not suitable for positive identification. It has been reported occasionally in whistling swans and is of an insignificant character in some trumpeters.) The feet are black but may show tints of brown, yellow or olive. Because the legs are somewhat longer than those of the mute swan the trumpeter walks more easily. Generally, the lores are black.

Although the whistling swan is slightly smaller than the trumpeter, it is difficult to distinguish between the two, since only rarely will one see the species together in such a way as to make valid size comparisons. Most, though not all, whistlers have a small patch of yellow in front of the eyes. Conversely, most trumpeters do not have such a yellow spot, though some do. Consequently, the presence of a yellow spot on the lores is not positive identification, but it is grounds for a reasonable assumption that the bird is a whistler. From a practical standpoint, the comparatively low population of trumpeters and their restricted range simplifies identification. Most black-billed swans seen in other locations will surely be whistlers.

Except for postmortem examination, surest identification is the voice. Trumpeters have a deep, resonant, hornlike call that reminds me of the way I think the hunting horns of ancient royalty would have sounded. Others have described the sound as being like the trumpet and horn fanfare of a symphony. The call of the whistling swan is different. I do not think "whistle" is properly descriptive, but I suppose it depends somewhat on the *kind* of whistle one has in mind.

As this is being written some 500 whistlers are feeding in a field near my home. I have been listening to their talk and wondering how best to describe it. It is difficult. The notes remind me of unaccented midrange notes on a flute.

The Latin name of the trumpeter was derived from its call. *Olor* means "a swan" a *buccinator* means "trumpeter." Commonly it may also be called wild swan or simply swan. In some localities it is called a bugler. On occasion, the name "whooper" is used; this undoubtedly causes some confusion with the true whooper species.

Most often one sees the trumpeter's neck held straight and the head high and alert, but I have spent many hours in a blind watching trumpeters that did not know I was there, and they frequently carried their necks in a graceful curve. However, the curve was never quite as pronounced as that of the mute, except when the trumpeters were feeding. Frequently, these birds lay the lower third of their necks against their backs between the wings with the upper two thirds bending abruptly, then standing straight up.

24

I have observed a great deal of head bobbing when several trumpeters are together. With its neck straight and its bill held horizontally, each bird dips its head with a graceful bend of the neck and quickly straightens it up again. The whole sequence consumes only a fraction of a second. The significance of this movement is obscure, but it appears to indicate tension of some sort.

These birds live in only a few localities in the northwestern United States, western Canada, southern and central Alaska.

South of Canada the largest population is in the Red Rock Lakes National Wildlife Refuge. Nearby, there are breeding trumpeters in Yellowstone National Park, Grand Teton National Park and the Island Park area of eastern Idaho. Some introductions have established small breeding populations in other areas—notably, the Malheur National Wildlife Refuge in eastern Oregon, Ruby Lake National Wildlife Refuge in northeastern Nevada and Lacreek National Wildlife Refuge in southern South Dakota.

In Alaska, the largest nesting populations are along the southern coast from Yakutat to Cordova and in the Copper River drainage. Trumpeters also nest in the Kantishna River valley southwest of Fairbanks, the Tanana Valley southeast of Fairbanks, the Susitna Valley northeast of Anchorage, the Yukon River delta and the Koyukuk Valley east of the Seward Peninsula. These northern trumpeters generally winter along the coast of southeastern Alaska and British Columbia. During severe winters some may move down to the southernmost parts of Vancouver Island.

There are small Canadian nesting populations in west-central Alberta (Grande Prairie region), southeastern Alberta and southwestern Saskatchewan. They apparently join late-migrating whistling swans and journey south to join the Red Rock Lakes trumpeter population that winters in Idaho on the open waters of Henry's Fork on the Snake River. Trumpeters tend to stay as near their breeding grounds as the

25

The whistling swan. Note the mark just in front of the eye. Most adult whistlers have this yellow mark.

weather permits and seldom travel any farther than is absolutely necessary to find food and open water.

Whistling Swan (*Olor columbianus*). The whistling swan is the common wild swan of North America. Colloquially, it is called whistler, wild swan, swan, cygne (swan), whooper and white swan. Since these names can be (and apparently have been) applied to the trumpeter, there is a great deal of confusion in the historical and localized reports of the whistling swan.

The whistler looks much like a small trumpeter, with the few visible differences previously mentioned. Weight, according to Kortright, is between 10 and 19 pounds. Trumpeters may be half again or even twice as heavy.

Whistling swans nest chiefly north of the Arctic Circle to about Latitude 79° North, from the Alaska Peninsula and the wet tundra margins of Kotzebue Sound, to Hudson Bay, Baffin Island and the Ungava Peninsula. Except for the concentrations on the Mackenzie and Anderson River deltas in Arctic Canada, these birds are scattered widely and thinly across the north country. They migrate to winter in Washington, Oregon, California, Nevada and Utah in the west; in the east they move along the Atlantic coast from the Chesapeake Bay to Currituck Sound, North Carolina. In rare instances, some may move on south into Florida and the Gulf coasts of Louisiana and Texas. They are casual visitors to Mexico and accidental visitors to Bermuda, Cuba, Puerto Rico and Newfoundland.

A recent estimate places the population of whistlers at around 100,000. Consequently, in the late fall and winter months any large concentration of swans (100 or more) seen south of Canada is certain to be whistlers. During the remainder of the year in this same area, there are mute swans, easily distinguished because of their orange-colored bill and the knob on the forehead, and trumpeters. A few whistlers are kept in zoos or parks for display, but these are nearly always identifiable from posted information.

Whooper Swan (*Olor cygnus*). The whooper, accidental and very rare in North America (Alaska and Maine), is a large bird (about the same size as the mute swan) with all-white plumage. Like the other

27

northern wild swans its plumage may also carry brown stains from the mineral content of the waters it inhabits. The eyes are brown; legs and feet are black. The chief distinguishing feature of this species is the bill. This has a tip of black, but the base of the bill (and lores) forward to the nostrils is lemon yellow. The bill has no knob, as does that of the mute, but is shaped like the bills of trumpeters and whistlers.

As its name suggests, the whooper is a noisy bird. In Russia it is referred to as the "calling swan." Its main call has been described as a loud, double bugle note with the second syllable pitched higher than the first. In addition, it has a loud single alarm call and lower conversational notes when feeding. It calls in flight as well as when on the ground, and a talkative flock makes a truly magnificent sound.

Russia has most of the world's whooper population, but small numbers breed in eastern Finland, northern Scotland and Scandinavia. In Iceland the whooper is widespread and common. Formerly, it was a nesting bird in southern Greenland, but now it seems to be found there only as a visitor, probably from Iceland. The Russian birds nest south of the tundra zone, sometimes as far as Latitude 45° North. During the winter, whoopers migrate to warmer climates. Winter concentrations may be found in the Caspian and Black Sea areas, and in central, south and southeast Asia. In Europe, wintering birds frequent southern Scandinavia, the British Isles, southern Spain, France and Italy. An occasional bird is reported from the Mediterranean coast of North Africa. Britain's wintering whoopers are primarily from Iceland.

Bewick's Swan (*Olor bewicki*). The smallest of the three species of swans native to Europe and Asia, Bewick's is sometimes called the tundra or small swan. Its coloration appears identical to that of the whooper, with the exception of the pattern of yellow-black on the bill. In whooper adults the area of yellow is much larger, extending in a wedge to below and beyond the nostril. The yellow on Bewick's is at the base of the bill only and terminates abruptly before it reaches the nostril.

If individuals of these two species can be seen together, the smaller size and shorter neck of the Bewick's swan is usually sufficient to identify it.

The voice is similar to the whistling swan's—somewhat softer and lower pitched, but pleasant and musical.

Bewick's swans nest along most of the northern coast of Scandinavia and Russia. In the winter they migrate southward to Holland, Den-

The whooper swan.

mark, Great Britain, the Black Sea, the Caspian Sea, west-central Asia, China, Japan and sometimes northern India.

In eastern Siberia there is a nesting population of similar swans that, according to some ornithologists, is a different race from Bewick's; they have given this bird the name "Jankowski's swan" (*Cygnus columbianus jankowskii*). I have found descriptions of only one real difference between the two races: the bill of Jankowski's swan is supposed to be larger and longer, broader near the tip and higher near the base than Bewick's. The yellow patch is also said to extend a little farther toward the nostrils and to be less bluntly truncated. So far this new classification has not received wide acceptance.

Bewick's swan. (Courtesy M. G. Preston, Bruce Coleman Ltd)

Meet the Swan

Black Swan (*Chenopis atratus*). Seeing my first black swan was a shock. Like most people I had grown up with the idea that all swans were the white ones that swim around on reflecting ponds garnished with water lilies. After I had a chance to get better acquainted with the black swan, however, I began to appreciate its beauty.

Smaller than the mute, this one has a long thin neck and an average wingspan of more than 6 feet. Its plumage is blackish. Each feather is also fringed with slate gray and has a white base, and the down is whitish. The bird has the unusual appearance of having feathers touched with frost. The primary and outer secondary (flight feathers) are white. Because of this coloration and their unusually long thin necks, black swans are especially strange and beautiful on the wing.

A pair of black swans.

The eyes are red. The bill, which has no frontal knob but is shaped like that of other swans, is crimson with a broad white band near the tip, which is also white. Legs and feet are blackish gray. The voice, high pitched and musical, is said to sound something like a toy trumpet.

The black swan is a native of Australia and though it lives predominately in the south, it occasionally is seen throughout the continent wherever there is water. There are concentration points where habitat conditions are more suitable: in Tasmania, along the southern coasts of New South Wales, Victoria, South Australia and in the south and west of West Australia. It prefers bodies of water either fresh or brackish with large surface areas. It also makes use of temporary floods and coastal rivers. The determining factor seems to be depth, since the birds cannot feed in water more than 3 feet deep.

The bird is not considered migratory (at least not in the same way as the whistler or Bewick's), but it seems to move considerable distances when stimulated by bad weather or a shortage of food.

No one knows how many black swans there are, but they are plentiful. Large concentrations—up to 50,000—have been reported. After they were introduced into Europe in the late eighteenth century black swans quickly became popular among waterfowl keepers and others interested in decorative birds. Later they were brought to America. Here they have also done well, though in this country none seems to have become established in a wild state as has the mute swan.

In New Zealand the situation is different. There, black swans were introduced in the latter half of the nineteenth century to control waterweeds, provide sport and be decorative as well. They found conditions to their liking and multiplied rapidly. Within a short period farmers were reporting damage to their crops and sportsmen were complaining of too many swans. Apparently the population has now been more or less stabilized by the regular taking of eggs and the shooting of adults. At Lake Ellesmere there are an estimated 60,000 to

80,000 swans that are regularly exploited commercially as a source of eggs and wildfowl meat.

Black-necked Swan *(Cygnus melancoriphus)*. The black-necked is the smallest of all the swans. Its long narrow body and pointed tail are pure white. The comparatively short neck and head are velvety black. The chin, however, is white, as is the line from the sides of the forehead up through the eyes to the nape. The eyes are dark brown. The bill, which is rather small, has a lead-gray tip, but the base and a large, fleshy, double-lobed frontal caruncle are scarlet.

These birds are not hesitant about expressing themselves vocally. On the ground, on the wing and when alarmed or excited they talk in a soft, musical whistle, quickly repeated.

The black-necked swan.

The black-necked swan is a South American bird that ranges throughout the south of the continent. Found in southern Brazil, Uruguay and Paraguay, it also lives in Chile south of Latitude 35° South, throughout Argentina south to Tierra del Fuego and in the Falkland Islands. North of Latitude 35° South it is a winter visitor only. Black-necked swans prefer open lakes, marshes or brackish lagoons and are usually more numerous near the coasts. Most of the time they gather in small flocks, but occasionally a few hundred may be seen.

In 1846 this species was first brought to Europe where the swans were valued for their uniqueness and decorative qualities. Black-necked swans are hardy birds able to withstand sub-zero temperatures if open water is available; therefore, they bred readily and adapted with little trouble. The birds have also been introduced into North America and have been successfully bred here. They are still fairly scarce, however, and I have had only a limited opportunity to observe them. Those that I have seen generally carried their necks in a graceful curve with the bill pointed downward at approximately a 45-degree angle.

Black-necked swans fly well and swiftly but get into the air with difficulty. On the other hand, they are not built for land travel—when grounded they waddle about even more awkwardly (or so it seems) than the much larger mute swan.

Coscoroba Swan (*Coscoroba coscoroba*). Although the Coscoroba swan is not generally considered a true swan, I have included it here because there is uncertainty about just what it is. I recently engaged in a rather lengthy debate with an official of a West Coast zoo as to whether or not it was a true swan. I am not sure I convinced him it was not.*

Editor's Note: Jean Delacour (*The Waterfowl of the World,* Vol. 1, p. 53) classifies the Coscoroba in the Tribe Anserini (swans and geese) and believes that "the very peculiar Coscoroba . . . is related to the Swans and to the whistling ducks. . . . Its true position [classification] still remains somewhat doubtful."

Meet the Swan

The Coscoroba resembles swans in color, size and some of its habits, but its general shape and proportions, its large feet and long legs (which enable it to walk on land with ease) and its comparatively rounded wings are reminiscent of the whistling ducks. It flies well and can rise straight from land or water without the long running takeoff required by the true swans.

The bird is pure white except for the six outer primary flight feathers, which are black on the outermost third of their length. The iris is whitish in adult males and dark brown in females and young

A pair of Coscoroba swans, which are not considered to be true swans.

birds. The eyelids are pink. The bill is a striking carmine crimson which looks almost artificial against the snow-white plumage. The nail at the tip of the bill is whitish. Unlike that of the true swans, the head is feathered in front of the eyes; because of this feature the bird somewhat resembles a goose. The legs and feet are light rosy pink. The female is noticeably smaller than the male.

Like the black-necked swan, the Coscoroba is a resident of southern Argentina, lives in the Falkland Islands, Tierra del Fuego, Chile, Uruguay, Paraguay and the extreme south of Brazil. It is usually seen either in small flocks of five or six (which undoubtedly represent a single family) or in groups of several families numbering 20 to 30 individuals, though occasionally the birds gather in flocks of 200 or 300.

The Coscoroba breeds in the south and winters in the northern part of its range. Since it is a bird of the Southern Hemisphere, where the seasons are the opposite of ours, it nests from September to December.

Spring

BY THE TIME spring officially arrives, most northern swans are well on the way to their breeding grounds. Usually a few overanxious birds rush the season and begin the northward movement only to face still-frozen country. There are reports of whistling swans arriving at Tule Lake, California, as early as February 20, when the lakes were still solidly frozen over. The ice did not begin to break up until nine days later. However, most migrating whistlers leave a bit later—usually in early March. At the Bear River Migratory Bird Refuge the population of northern-bound birds peaks late in March, but concentrations are never so large as during fall. Perhaps this is an indication that the northern route (or at least the points or duration of stopover) is not the same as in the spring.

Throughout March, April and early May the swans leave Bear River to continue their northern journey. Those that winter on the East Coast follow approximately the same timetable as they migrate northward. Some reach southern Canada in late March or early April and some touch the Arctic coast as early as May 4. Most whistlers, however, arrive in the western Arctic after mid-May and do not reach the eastern Arctic until somewhat later. Some may still be on migration as late as mid-June.

Whistlers that arrive early in the Arctic occupy whatever open water they can find. Usually this will be at the edge of ice floes at sea. Bad weather at this time may cause them considerable distress. Even when they finally reach the tundra there will usually still be a great amount of snow and ice present. Pairs scatter out over the bleak land, each pair claiming a breeding territory on the low tundra. Usually the chosen sites are on the borders of marshy lakes or on islands, but sometimes they may be quite far from water.

The Eurasian whooper swans, similarly inclined to start north early, may reach the nesting areas under winter conditions. Spring cold snaps and snowstorms may send the birds back southward to wait for better weather.

Whistler pairs take possession of their chosen sites with a great deal of calling and displaying, often on land. With arched necks and outstretched wings they walk about bowing and bobbing their extended necks up and down. During this period the pairs are extremely hostile toward other swans, and each pair claims a rather extensive territory. Where whistling swan density is greatest (in Canada along the coastal strip from the west side of the Mackenzie delta to the east side of the Anderson delta) there is approximately one pair to each square mile. Farther inland, in those areas where the terrain is suitable for nesting, the density is less.

Trumpeters, whoopers, mute swans and black-necked swans are also intensely intolerant of other swans during the nesting period, and each pair patrols a sizable territory. On the other hand, black swans and Bewick's swans are colonial, or substantially so, in their nesting habitats. Small lakes in trumpeter or whooper territory are usually occupied by only one pair, whereas black swans may nest within 5 to 10 feet of one another. *Birds of the Soviet Union* (Vol. IV, Georges P. Dementiev and N. A. Gladkov, editors) described a 1950 Bewick's breeding area where "several dozen (nesting pairs) could be seen at any time in any direction."

Although the North American whistling swan is far more plentiful than the trumpeter, it has been largely unstudied, probably because

A pair of mute swans feeding together.

its breeding grounds are scattered thinly across the Arctic wilderness in a virtually unpeopled land. The trumpeter, on the other hand, which has been precariously balanced on the edge of oblivion for more than 50 years, has lived under the watchful eyes of conservationists. Its territorial activities, especially on the Red Rock Lakes National Wildlife Refuge have therefore been well documented.

Like the whistling swans, trumpeters seem impatient to occupy their breeding grounds in the spring; at Red Rock they have been seen in midwinter far out in the vast snowfields that cover the breeding habitat. By April, when water from melted snow edges the ice covering of the lakes, the birds are ready to move in. Activity on the thawing marsh increases with rising spring temperatures. Swans alone, in pairs and in groups move about restlessly, trumpeting far into the night.

Practically nothing is known about relationships between young unpaired wild swans or about their first pair formations. Some writers contend that pairing takes place during the third year. However, the Lacreek National Wildlife Refuge in South Dakota reports that among trumpeters relocated there, pair formation occurred during the swans' second year and some swans paired when only 14 months old. In Lacreek, also, trumpeters were reported nesting at the age of two years, nine months.

Whether this early breeding age is simply a case of precocious birds or whether (as has been suggested) it is due to the availability of ample nesting territory on this refuge is not known. In general, three to four years is the accepted age at which swans mature. But some swans may not nest for the first time until they are five or six years old. There are indications that a late breeding age may be the result of the occupation of a limited area by high populations of mature birds, since in this situation young birds find it difficult to obtain suitable nesting territory. For example, data from Red Rock Lakes shows increased cygnet production accompanying an increase in the size of the adult population until the number of swans reaches what is apparently a habitat saturation point; then reproduction begins to decline.

Owen Vivion, former refuge manager at Red Rock Lakes, told me of three-year-old trumpeters that attempted to nest but were unsuccessful. In another situation involving trumpeters of that age, the female laid eggs but did not incubate them successfully. Eventually, the pair abandoned the nest. A later examination showed the eggs to be infertile.

Both black swans and mute swans are reported to have bred at the age of two years, but this seems to be unusual. A breeding age of three to five years is more common. It is likely that as regards breeding age all swans follow much this same pattern.

For all Northern Hemisphere swans pair formation apparently takes place during the fall. No elaborate displays are involved. The birds swim near each other, pressing the plumage close to the body and carrying their necks and heads high.

Later, when the swans mature and are ready for breeding, more elaborate courting takes place and is repeated each year in late winter and early spring as the mating instinct asserts itself. Owen Vivion described how at this time of the year trumpeter pairs indulged in much head and neck rubbing.

In courtship the trumpeter swan most commonly displays itself by raising its partially extended wings until they are horizontal and then holding them, quivering, in that position. This pose is accompanied by much trumpeting, with the head held high and the neck extended vertically. It is mostly a display of aggression toward another swan, but it may involve four or five birds in a group demonstration and may also follow the successful repelling of an invading swan. In the latter case the male usually returns to his mate and the two indulge in a mutual display of triumph. First the male trumpeter announces the conquest with loud trumpeting. Then after the female acknowledges with a staccato reply, they salute each other with outstretched quivering wings and with a dipping of the head. The ceremony is concluded with long wailing cries.

The precopulatory display involves repeated dipping of the head and neck into the water by both birds, a sequence that is terminated by four or five synchronized dipping movements. During the last one the male may cross his neck over that of the female. When ready to accept the male, the female flattens herself in the water with her neck half extended.

Mute swans follow a similar pattern of actions. After copulation, they arch their necks stiffly, rear up breast to breast, utter an odd snoring note, then sink back down.

I have found no mention of swans hybridizing under wild conditions, probably because there is little, if any, overlapping in breeding territories. There are known crosses between captive birds, however, where trumpeters paired off with whistling swans, mute swans and Canada geese. Johnsgard, in his *Handbook of Waterfowl Behavior*, states that Bewick's and whistling swans have hybridized with trumpeters, whoopers, mutes and black swans. Apparently the black-necked swan has never crossed with any other species.

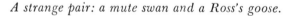

A strange pair: a mute swan and a Ross's goose.

Spring

One spring at the Portland, Oregon, zoo, I saw what appeared to be an unusual pair formation attempted in the waterfowl pool—between a mute swan and a Ross's goose. I could not tell which was male and which was female, nor could I determine if the attraction was mutual. In any event, the Ross's goose trailed the much larger bird as if afraid it might escape.

Sometime after the spring ice breakup, paired trumpeters take over their territories and begin defending them against other swans. For a

A trumpeter gives another swan a blow with its bill. Other than the loss of a few feathers, usually little damage is done.

trumpeter a territory is the mating, nesting and feeding ground for the young. If an intruding swan approaches, the resident pair display their wings aggressively and trumpet a warning to the would-be trespasser. If the warning is ignored, the defending male is quick to attack.

Several years ago I had a pair of trumpeters under observation on Knox Pond in the Malheur National Wildlife Refuge. The pond was roughly a half mile long and a quarter mile wide and had a considerable growth of emergent water plants on the east and south sides. Suddenly the pair of swans broke into a strident trumpeting. As I looked around for the cause of this disturbance an intruding pair of swans swung in front of me and braked to a landing on the pond, several hundred yards from the resident pair. They were obviously trespassers. Incensed at this disregard of their warnings, the local birds took off and flew toward them. The intruders quickly moved to the far side of the pond. This, however, was not enough to satisfy the first pair, which circled around and came on again. Finally convinced that they were not wanted, the latecomers took off and left the pond to its original claimants. This seems to be the normal result of such encounters, with the resident pair emerging victorious.

The mute swan is extremely aggressive while nesting. Because, for the most part, these birds have been raised under semidomesticated conditions in this country, they have little fear of man and will attack when the nest is threatened. Often the attack will be broken off at the water's edge if the intruder is on dry land, probably because the swan feels at a disadvantage out of the water.

Nevertheless, one time while I was photographing a nesting pair on the millpond in Bend, Oregon, the male bird came some 20 or 30 feet out of the water and chased a friend, William Van Allen, who had to step lively to get out of the old male's line of fire. The nest itself, with the female sitting on the eggs, was some 10 yards from shore and was partially concealed by high emergent growth. Obviously the male was not satisfied with a 30-foot moat. He started after us when we were still 100 feet away and came plowing through the water, propelled by strong, simultaneous thrusts of his large webbed feet, pushing a substantial "bow" wave ahead.

While on the water, the male carried his neck arched and laid back tight against the back, and the bill pointed downward so that it touched the neck. He raised the upper joints of the wings and elbows

At close range an angry mute male is an imposing sight. This one was intent on driving us away because we were too close to his nest.

above his back, lifting the stiff, curved, secondary flight feathers so that they arched up and outward. He was, indeed, an imposing sight.

We felt certain that the bird would stop when he reached the shore and, in fact, he did hesitate for some seconds as if uncertain about his next move. But when Van Allen approached too close, the male's mind was made up—to come storming ashore after him. Despite the swan's awkwardness and one pinioned wing, he was surprisingly fast. My friend was lucky to escape, though it is doubtful that under the circumstances the bird could have inflicted anything worse than a few minor bruises.

After leaving the water, the swan assumed a different threat posture. He extended his wings slightly, curving the neck forward so that the head pointed down and the bill was pressed against the lowest part of the neck. Apparently, this stance allowed him to strike with his wings or his neck, or with all together.

The black swan also has a conspicuous threat display. It raises its secondary flight feathers as does the mute swan, but instead of carrying its neck curved low and its head back, the black swan keeps the neck erect (except for the top part, which is sharply bent). It also ruffles its long neck feathers and carries the bill pointed slightly downward.

Although it is the smallest, the black-necked is the most aggressive of all swans. It keeps its wings close to its body when threatening an attack and swims toward its "enemy" with the neck outstretched. Actual fighting is done with the wings.

Except for some observations on trumpeters, not much is known about the relationship between swans and other species of birds that share their breeding area. It might be presumptuous to assume that other swan species have similar habits, but I have found no indication to the contrary. Possibly, the smaller and more hostile black-necked swan, or the black swan, might have different patterns of behavior.

Trumpeters pay little attention to ducks or coots. I have seen coots feeding within a few feet of an occupied trumpeter nest and neither the female sitting on the nest nor the male feeding nearby showed any concern. Also ignored are small birds and ducks nesting within a few yards of a swan's nest. Geese and larger water birds are not so

Bill Van Allen barely escaped when the angry swan came out of the water to continue the chase.

welcome; these the trumpeter often drives away. But this intolerance is confined to nesting territories. Prior to the nesting season, paired trumpeters on the Malheur Refuge fed peacefully in mixed crowds of snow geese, Canada geese and ducks.

Ducks and coots sometimes compete with impunity for food particles that the parent swans bring to the surface for the cygnets. Not, of course, that an irritated swan may never take a poke with its bill at an especially persistent coot, but this is hardly outright aggression.

Captive mute swans sometimes display a worse temper toward other inhabitants of park ponds, but more than likely this is the result of a crowding of waterfowl in too small an area. In my experience the only attacks on other waterfowl species by mute swans occurred while park visitors were feeding the birds food scraps. At such times the

Muskrats are important to trumpeters because muskrat houses make excellent nesting sites.

mute swan would punish a careless duck or goose with a hard blow from its bill. I once saw a day-old mallard killed almost instantly by a swan that was annoyed at the tiny bird for stealing a bread crumb.

Lethal attacks from swans are rare, but a Yellowstone Park trumpeter is said to have killed a muskrat that was threatening its cygnets.

The trumpeter treats larger mammals with more respect, and when such an intruder—a man, for example—approaches a nest or young, the adult birds are quick to leave.

Territorial establishment and defense begin sometime before the nest is constructed and continue into late summer when the cygnets are half grown. These activities are most common during nesting and early brooding and then begin to taper off. It appears, however, that after the territories have been well established, each pair tends to respect the rights of the others and there is little tendency to trespass. That conflicts are rare enables the birds to attend to the incubation and care of the young as well as their own feeding—and maybe a bit of loafing.

Nonbreeders also learn to stay away from breeding territories. They spend their time far out from shore where extensive underwater aquatic plants provide them with food, or they loaf along shorelines unclaimed by breeding pairs.

Good trumpeter nesting territory apparently has certain well-defined characteristics, although naturalists may not yet know of all of them. That some locations are more desirable than others probably accounts for the return by the same pairs year after year to the same sites, even the same nests. Nor is this just a nostalgic attraction to an old "home," as is indicated by the fact that if a territory should go unclaimed, another pair quickly moves in. On the other hand, land that looks the same (to human eyes) as occupied trumpeter territory may go untenanted.

In his monograph *The Trumpeter Swan*, Winston E. Banko outlines some of the specific physical features of this swan's breeding-habitat requirements. They are:

"1. Stable waters possessing a relatively static level, not exhibiting marked seasonal fluctuations.

"2. Quiet waters of lake, marsh, or slough, not waters subject to obvious current or constant wave action.

"3. Shallow waters of lake or open marsh, not so deep as to preclude considerable digging and foraging for lower aquatic plant parts, roots, tubers, etc."

Within a territory that meets these requirements, the birds look for a certain amount of privacy. In areas where there are irregular shorelines and numerous small islands, swans will nest closer together than where shorelines are relatively straight. In Red Rock Lakes where habitats of both types exist, a territory of 70 acres per nesting pair along the irregular shores was enough, as compared to 150 acres per pair where the shorelines were more or less straight.

This desire for privacy is one of the principal factors limiting trumpeter reproduction. As the population of breeding birds increases in a given area there is little, if any, reduction in territorial demands. New pairs must either use unsuitable nesting sites or encroach upon established pairs—with all the conflict that accompanies such an invasion. In either case, nesting usually results in less reproduction, despite the larger breeding population.

The trumpeter population that breeds near Grande Prairie, in the Peace River district of Alberta, has remained fairly constant at around 100 birds. The controlling factor seems to be a shortage of the sort of habitat into which an increased population might expand, and the large amount of space required for each breeding pair. One lake of some 1,500 acres accommodates only two pairs. Each of the other pairs are the lone occupants of lakes up to 800 acres in size.

Also, there must be a certain amount of water space in a trumpeter's territory, apparently to satisfy landing and takeoff requirements. Since they cannot serve this purpose, small potholes, even those containing an abundance of food, are of little value to swans.

Spring

The focal point of each swan pair's territory is the nesting site. Muskrat houses are the favorite nesting site at Red Rock Lakes, where abandoned beaver lodges are also used. Since trumpeters appreciate the safety afforded by water they often choose sites (like these) that are partially or completely surrounded by it. In Yellowstone National Park, where the terrain is quite different, swans generally use small islands in the various lakes as nest sites, though an occasional nest will be built on a lake shore in an open and unconcealed area.

Whistling swans seem to prefer small islands in shallow tundra ponds but may choose sites on the top of low hills as much as a half mile from water. They choose spots that are free of snow and that will be above spring snow-pool level.

Whoopers favor large lakes with islands but may also nest along the shores of slow-moving rivers.

A mute swan on its nest. Note the neck position.

The semidomesticated mute swan may nest anywhere at ground level either near water or on the water. The nests I have seen were usually located where there was some protection from intruders. Volume IV of *Birds of the Soviet Union* (Georges P. Dementiev and N. A. Gladkov, editors) tells of nests that lie in "inaccessible reedbeds" or on "floating vegetation."

Black swans nest in reedbeds or on land (usually a small island), but their nests have also been found on the tops of flooded stumps and in masses of floating debris.

Bewick's swans nest in the estuaries of large rivers in Arctic Russia where there is swampy, grass-covered, low-lying tundra, and numerous open lakes.

Black-necked swans build their nests among rushes in or near shallow water. The nests are built up from the bottom of the marsh to a height of 4 or 5 feet, and the tops, sometimes as wide as 2 feet in diameter, rise about a foot out of the water. The birds approach and leave their nests by swimming.

In general, all swans build large bulky nests of the available plant material near the nest site. At some often-used sites the nest is added to year after year and may reach gigantic proportions. One such nest (a whistling swan's) was 6 feet in diameter and from 2 to 3 feet in height. Swans do not carry nesting material to the nest site but may pick it up and toss it, with a sidewise movement of the head and neck, in the general direction of the nest. Down seems to be a major lining material in the nests of some species, but others use it little if at all. Whoopers, Bewick's and mute swans use down; whistlers, trumpeters, blacks and black-necks apparently do not, although some feathers may be mixed in with the nesting material.

Both trumpeter sexes help to build the nest, but apparently the female does most of the work. Basically, construction appears to be a matter of gathering all the grasses, sedges, reeds, and so on, within neck-stretching distance and piling them up. Nests built on sites previously used need little more than shaping since much of the nest material may already be in position. Conversely, nests constructed on relatively barren ground may be little more than hollowed-out earthen forms.

I spent an afternoon watching trumpeters that were nesting on a small lake in the Grand Teton National Park. The nest was about 30 feet from shore on a mound of rushes that probably started out as a muskrat house. Since it was the second week in June and some Teton trumpeters were already showing off their new cygnets, the eggs in this nest could be expected to hatch at any time. It appeared to be in good shape; nevertheless, the patient female spent much of her time shaping and rebuilding. She would reach out as far as her long neck

This trumpeter's nest is located about 30 feet from shore on a small lake.

would permit, get a billful of nesting material, and place it near the top of the nest at her side.

In the meantime, the male, which was feeding nearby, occasionally spent several minutes picking up floating bits of old weeds and dropping them "over his shoulder" in the direction of the nest. Since he was then at least 10 feet away, it is unlikely that any of this material ever reached the nest. However, the activity was an indication that the building instinct carries on late into the nesting season.

Because of the weather egg laying starts earlier in the south than it does in the north. The mute swans I watched for so many years in Bend, Oregon, were generally finished with the laying of eggs in late March or early April. At Red Rock Lakes most trumpeter clutches are completed by May 15. In southern Alaska trumpeters start laying a few days later, while up along the Arctic Ocean, whistling swans (and probably whoopers and Bewick's) start laying much later, probably in late May or early June.

The nesting season of the black-necked swan appears to be somewhat variable, but it usually nests from July to November, according to location and circumstances. In their South American home country, of course, late winter and early spring nesting would occur during these months.

The black swan is even more unscheduled; it may not nest at all if weather conditions are unfavorable. However, laying usually begins in June or July in South Australia and somewhat later in New Zealand, where it is generally completed by early December. Adult black swans fail to hatch or rear the young when water is scarce. On the other hand, they react quickly to any rainfall and may nest almost any time of the year, provided that there is adequate water. Captive black swans will readily breed throughout the year. As a matter of fact, in captivity both black and black-necked swans will produce two or three clutches of eggs in one year if the eggs are removed after each clutch is completed.

From the left: a trumpeter's egg, a Canada goose egg, and an ordinary domestic hen's egg.

Trumpeters, whistlers, whoopers and mute swans lay one egg every other day. Black swans lay an egg about every day or day and a half. The laying rate for black-necked and Bewick's swans is not known, but since they are both smaller birds, they probably produce an egg approximately every 24 hours. Possibly the interval is a bit longer.

Incubation usually begins after the last egg is laid. However, it is known that trumpeters leaving a nest with the first cygnets hatched have abandoned eggs containing well-developed embryos, an indication that all eggs did not start to incubate at the same time.

The trumpeter's average clutch contains four to six eggs, but as many as nine may be laid. When laid the eggs are somewhat granular in texture and off-white in color. They measure about $4\frac{1}{3}$ inches by $2\frac{7}{8}$ inches. Like all swans' eggs they pick up a stain (often brownish) after

55

incubation begins. According to Banko and Mackay, they hatch in 32 or 33 days.

Whistling swans produce a clutch of two to seven creamy white eggs measuring, on the average, 4¼ inches by 2⅔ inches. These hatch in 35 to 40 days.

The whooper's four to six eggs are also creamy white. In size they are about as large as the trumpeter's, and take about the same length of time to hatch.

The mute swan lays a somewhat larger egg, 4½ inches by 3 inches,

A male mute swan stands guard while the female incubates the eggs.

that is grayish or bluish; clutches average four to seven, but may comprise as many as 12 eggs. Incubation takes from 35 to 38 days, usually 35.

Bewick's swan, smaller than the other white swans, lays a grayish-white egg 4$\frac{1}{10}$ inches by 2$\frac{3}{5}$ inches in clutches of two to five. Incubation requires 34 to 38 days.

Black swans lay pale-green eggs in clutches of four to eight. These eggs are 4$\frac{1}{2}$ inches by 2$\frac{3}{5}$ inches and incubate in about 39 days.

The black-necked swan lays four to seven eggs that measure

A mute swan doing a bit of housekeeping.

This four-picture sequence shows a pair of mute swans changing places on the nest. I think the male is on the nest in the first photograph.

4$\frac{1}{10}$ inches by 2$\frac{3}{5}$ inches and are smooth, glossy and cream colored. They hatch in 34 to 36 days.

There is some uncertainty as to whether or not the male swan assists in the incubation. In the wild it is difficult to determine whether male or female is on the nest. However, the scarcity of positive reports of males covering the eggs would indicate that incubation is primarily a function of the female. Black swan and mute swan pairs have been reported to share the chore. One pair of captive whistlers was also said to take turns on the nest during a period of hot weather, but on cooler days the male left the job to the female. On the whole, dividing the labors in this way is apparently rare.

Summer

THE KNOBBY CRESTS of the Centennial Mountains, white with new snow, stood out starkly against the ominous black clouds of the advancing storm. For a few brief moments, the mid-June sun forced its way through the darkness, and a bright circle, as from some giant spotlight, moved across the valley floor. Its brilliance touched the white-capped waters of Upper Red Rock Lake, crossed the wind-whipped shoreline and moved on. Before the sun surrendered to the charging storm, a distant white spot flashed briefly and disappeared. Through the spotting scope the white spot became a trumpeter swan patiently sitting on its nest.

It was cold. Gale-force winds drove a fine chilly rain that felt like icy needles against my face and which, at this altitude—6,600 feet—could easily turn to sleet or snow. It was June 16, and therefore this swan, like the others nesting on the Red Rock Lakes Migratory Waterfowl Refuge, probably had been sitting on her eggs for a month or more. Although summer was near, bad weather persisted. I wondered how many such storms the female had endured, her bill tucked under a wing as snow beat at her and drifted around the nest. And what about the whistlers, whoopers and Bewick's in the far north on frozen tundra, an area that is inhospitable even in midsummer?

Undoubtedly, nesting pairs, and especially the females, face many hardships during the long and tedious incubation period.

A graceful female trumpeter sitting patiently on her nest.

After the excitement of the mating season and the physical demands of egg laying, incubation probably settles quickly into a routine of sitting on the eggs, housekeeping and nest repair, preening and feeding.

Earlier I mentioned a pair of nesting trumpeters I had watched in Grand Teton National Park. Altogether I spent most of one day near this nest and so was able to get an impression of the daily activities of these birds. (I should add, however, that this pair had nested on a small lake where there were no other swans or large water birds nearby. For this reason I did not see any nest defense by the male.)

When I first arrived, I moved with great caution to a slight rise overlooking the lake. I was not sure exactly where the nest was, and all my previous experience with these swans had shown that they are extremely wary. The last thing I wanted to do was to frighten them away from their nest. Fortunately, when I peeked over the hill and

After feeding, the female spent several minutes preening before sitting on her eggs again.

saw them, they were still 150 yards away. All the time expecting some reaction from the pair, I then mounted the camera and long telephoto on the tripod.

At this point, the female apparently became aware of me for the first time and hurriedly left the nest. She must have decided I meant no harm, however, for a few moments later she climbed back upon the nest mound. The male, swimming nearby, seemed only casually interested in the whole affair. The female did not return to the eggs immediately but spent several minutes beside the nest, preening. Next she poked around in the nest bowl as if moving the eggs about (but I could not see down inside the nest). Then she settled carefully on the eggs with a sort of squirming motion.

A few minutes later she moved a few pieces of nesting material toward the top of the nest. After another short interval she got to her feet. Apparently she did not like the arrangement, for she again poked into the nest with her bill, rearranging something; she settled down finally, after turning 180 degrees from her previous position.

By this time the pair was apparently accustomed to my presence. I moved slowly toward them. Eventually, after an hour of inching forward, always in their view, I had the tripod standing 20 feet from the lake's edge and within 50 feet of the nest. The female sat calmly on the eggs. The male stood a few feet down the shoreline on the other side of a clump of bushes and preened. I am fairly sure that the lack of concern at my nearness was due, not to my great stalking ability, but to the

Left: Through a screen of bushes, the male watched me.

Opposite: The female appeared to be covering her eggs before leaving the nest to feed.

fact that somewhere in their past these birds had learned to know people and had not been frightened by them.

Most of the time while I was there the male stayed within 20 or 30 feet of the nest, but at no time did he climb upon the nest mound. He made one expedition that took him some 50 yards away, but I could see no reason for it except his search for food.

The female left the nest again that afternoon, but first she stood up and spent several minutes working on its interior. She circled the bowl as she worked, and though I could not see exactly what she was doing, it appeared that she might be raking nesting material over the eggs to protect them. Satisfied, finally, she slipped into the water and began feeding nearby. I did not time this feeding period, but it seemed to last 15 to 20 minutes.

Other observers have described this egg-covering activity, which serves to protect the eggs from heat or cold as well as from the view of predators. Apparently, all Northern Hemisphere swans cover the eggs when leaving the nest. The only exception to this would be the mute swan at times when the male takes over the incubation chore. On the other side of the world, black swans take turns on the nest,

Part of preening includes a vigorous body shake.

but the female black-necked swan, which does all the sitting, simply goes away to feed and leaves the eggs uncovered. In this case, the male stays close by to guard the nest while she is gone.

When my female trumpeter returned to the nest, the usual preening period followed; then she settled back onto the eggs. Instead of using the bill to remove the covering of nest material from the eggs, she seemed to shove it off with a side-to-side body motion. While on the nest, she frequently rested by laying her head back on her body, and seemed to take short naps with her bill tucked under one wing.

The nesting activities of a female whooper swan in Scotland were described as similar to the trumpeter's.

During the incubation period the male trumpeter stays near the nest to protect it against intruders. However, once nesting territories are well established, he has only minor police duties to perform. The pair seldom leave their territory during this time. Occasionally, one of the birds may make a defensive flight or may rise to take a quick look around. Such flights may extend to some neutral territory where the bird (whether alone or with others of its kind) may feed or loaf without conflict. Should these swans' lines of flight pass near the nests of others, the resident pairs will advise the trespasser of this fact with suitable aggressive warning displays.

When the young trumpeter is ready to hatch, it breaks its way through the eggshell by means of an egg tooth, a sharp point on the tip of the upper mandible. Breaking out is exhausting work for the young swan, because the shell is about $\frac{1}{25}$ inch thick and is very strong.

Trumpeter eggs at Red Rock Lakes normally hatch between June 15 and June 25. The hatching is probably progressively later the farther north it occurs. Hatching at Red Rock has not been spectacularly successful. The percentage has been low in comparison to that of lesser waterfowl; in some studies it has ranged from 51 to 66 percent. Trumpeter studies on the Kenai Peninsula, Alaska, reported a 65-percent hatching success.

Infertility of eggs and death of embryos cause most losses in the nesting stage, but little is known about the reasons for each. Frequently, the embryo dies after it is well developed, possibly because incubation began before all the eggs were laid and the female left the nest with the cygnets that hatched first. Chilling of the embryo may also be fatal if the female leaves the nest for too long during inclement weather.

Predation, however, does not account for much egg loss at Red Rock Lakes and may not be an important factor in other nesting areas.

Since, in general, incubation of all eggs begins at the same time, the cygnets hatch at nearly the same time, or at least within 48 hours.

For a short time after hatching, the young swans rest while their

67

A baby mute swan comes out to get acquainted with its mother.

One of the cygnets tries to climb under its mother's wing.

When the female swan got up, I could see that one of the eggs had not yet hatched.

One of the cygnets trails its mother to the water's edge.

covering of fine down dries out. The tiny birds are precocial. That is, they are clothed in down, their eyes are open and functioning and, as soon as they are dry, they can run or swim and feed themselves. Newly hatched trumpeters weigh 7 to 7½ ounces. Cygnets of other species are of a comparable size or a bit smaller. All look much the same.

The downy young of the trumpeter has been described as having a gray phase (common) and a white phase (rare). Both colors may occur in the same brood. In the gray phase the head and neck are mouse gray; the body is mouse gray over the back and lighter gray to white on the underside. Feet are yellowish; the bill is pinkish at its base and dark gray near the tip. In the white phase the plumage is white, the feet yellowish and the bill flesh colored.

Young whistlers are white but are tinged with buff to ivory yellow on the head, neck and breast, whereas the bill and feet are fleshy pink.

The downy whooper and Bewick's are pale-grayish white above and white below, with darker areas on the crown, nape, shoulders and rump. Bill and feet are flesh colored.

Although destined to be opposite colors as adults, black swans and mute swans start out looking alike, a fairly uniform light gray above and white below. The bills are black and the feet a brownish gray. On the downy mute there is no indication of the knob at the base of the bill that develops in adults.

The black-necked cygnet is almost pure white—there is only the faintest of gray tints above. Its bill and feet are black.

The length of time a wild trumpeter female broods her newly hatched cygnets is not known, but if the actions of captive trumpeters are an indication, she spends many daylight hours on the nest warming the young. She continues this at night for quite a long time. In a family of wild trumpeters kept under observation for some ten days, the female brooded the young at night, on rainy days and often after they returned from long excursions. It is probably safe to assume that whistlers, whoopers and Bewick's swans take equally good care of their young.

70

Summer

Owen Vivion told me of cygnet losses at Red Rock that resulted from unseasonably cold weather at a time when the young cygnets were not being brooded. He estimated that 60 to 70 percent of the hatch was lost, primarily because of this chilling.

Mute, black and black-necked swans have their own distinctive method of brooding. Often the females take the young birds onto their backs. The young can then move under the wings for warmth or protection. Black-necked cygnets are extremely shy and spend their first two or three weeks riding around on the backs of the parents, hidden

One cygnet has already lost the down from its lores; the other's is still covered.

under the wings. They come out to feed but scamper back to safety if disturbed.

Parent trumpeters are solicitous of the welfare of the cygnets, especially during the first few weeks after hatching. At this time the adults more or less keep the young birds between them; when moving, the cygnets follow the lead bird, usually the female, while the other adult brings up the rear.

As a rule parent trumpeters do not carry cygnets on their backs. But, as happens so often with wildlife, there are exceptions. One occurred when a pair of trumpeters with five cygnets in the Lacreek National Wildlife Refuge was surprised by an observer. As the swan family moved away from the disturbance, the cygnets swam between the parent birds. One cygnet, possibly a tired one, swam around behind an adult, climbed onto its back, sat down and started preening. The parents disregarded this unusual action. After riding for five minutes the cygnet rejoined the brood, and the family moved off into a growth of cattails.

A family of mute swans.

While an adult mute swan preens, its cygnet rests on the ground and picks at its down in a similar manner. A porcelain sculpture featuring the mute swan as a new peace symbol was presented to Chairman Mao Tse-tung by President Nixon during his historic visit to China in February, 1972.

The World of the Swan

As might be expected, the early weeks of cygnets' lives are the most hazardous. The parents may trample the young in their clumsiness, and though the young are born knowing how to swim, they may become entangled in water plants and drown. Leeches attack some, and internal parasites others. An English study disclosed that approximately 50 percent of the mute cygnets in the study area had died before they reached the age of flight.

If a trumpeter family appears to be threatened by the presence of humans, adult birds will usually desert the young without any effort to protect them. However, if they have an opportunity, they may lead the flotilla of cygnets into a dense growth of emergent water plants, such as reeds, bulrushes or cattails, to hide before they leave the area. Trumpeters of all ages will dive underwater to avoid danger. Older cygnets get quite good at this. Whenever possible the adults avoid danger by flight, but during their summer flightless period they either flounder along on top of the water or submerge. Sometimes, to remain

Three coots and a drake mallard wait to pick up the scraps as a trumpeter swan feeds.

concealed, they pull their bodies underwater, apparently by some special swimming action with their feet, and leave only their heads above water. No doubt this is fairly effective, especially when the bird is already partly concealed by weed growth, but the action consumes a lot of energy, and it is not likely that the bird can hide like this for any great length of time.

An undisturbed family of trumpeters spends most of the day swimming, loafing and feeding. Feeding, in particular, takes a lot of time. Since the young must increase their weight some 30 times within about 100 days to reach flight stage, cygnets especially always seem to be looking for something to eat.

The first foods of trumpeter cygnets are mostly aquatic beetles, other insects and crustaceans. There are two probable reasons for this preponderance of animal matter in their early diets. First, since animal matter contains more nourishment in a given amount than does vegetable matter, it may have great survival value by furnishing the young birds with concentrated food values during their first critical weeks of life. Second, during this period aquatic plant growth is just beginning, and therefore the young, tender plant parts that are suitable for young birds are not yet available.

Food items are brought to the surface by the adult birds as they probe their bills at the mud and underwater growth, or stir up bottom material by treading vigorously with their powerful legs and strong webbed toes. Holes over a foot deep and several feet in diameter result from this activity; they can often be seen in the shallow waters of Red Rock Lakes. In the Malheur National Wildlife Refuge, trumpeters searching for roots and sprouts along shorelines and riverbanks undermined the banks by gouging out the earth with bills powered by stout muscular necks.

After about a month or so, cygnets cut down on the animal matter in their diets and begin feeding primarily on aquatic plants in deeper water. During this period their food-hunting skills improve, and they

75

In deep water the trumpeter tips up in order to reach desirable underwater vegetation.

depend less on their parents and more upon their own abilities. By the time the cygnets are two or three months old, they eat about the same things as the parents.

The food of all swan species is largely plants, and all probably obtain it in much the same manner as the trumpeter. I have already mentioned the methods of stirring up the bottom mud and gathering underwater vegetation with the bill and long neck, but there is another. If the water is a bit too deep, the trumpeter may "tip up" like a mallard duck to reach the food.

I have never had an underwater look at a tipped-up swan, but if it feeds with its neck stretched straight down, it must be able to reach plants approximately 3½ feet below the surface. Trumpeters apparently never dive for food; diving is used only to escape danger. Consequently, if the water is too deep for the birds to reach food items by tipping up, they look elsewhere.

76

Summer

Although most of their feeding is confined to water, on rare occasions both immature and adult trumpeters may move out onto land to graze. I have seen whistling swans feeding in a cutover cornfield only a few miles from my home in Oregon's central Willamette Valley. They stayed there several days; I assume they were gathering waste corn (but did not check on it because I had no desire to disturb the flock). I also saw a pair of whistlers walking around in a pasture on Sauvie's Island west of Portland, Oregon, but they had seen me first and started to walk away. As a result I had no chance to determine whether or not they had been grazing on meadow grass. In early December, 1970, 100 whistlers fed in a field across the road from my home. They were still there in mid-January, but by then they had been joined by 400 more. The attraction appeared to be new green plant growth.

Tubers and roots, along with the stems and leaves, of various aquatic plants are staple food items. The swans reported by Lewis and Clark as eating the root of the wapato or duck potato may have been either

A pair of whistlers feed on meadow grass.

whistling swans or trumpeters. Another early source also observed trumpeters eating this food. In addition, they feed on pondweed, water milfoil, muskgrass, waterweed, duckweed, tules, spatterdock, bur reed, filamentous green algae, sedge spikes, sago pondweed, white water buttercup, mare's tails, water moss, and so on.

In captivity trumpeter swans have been fed barley and wheat, also used as a winter food supplement for the wild birds on Red Rock Lakes. When eating grain or weed seeds, swans also take in a certain amount of grit. Bulk green foods in large quantities appear to be important for reproduction. Mr. C. L. Cunningham, a successful breeder of swans in Woodinville, Washington, fed his birds great quantities of fresh lawn clippings and considered them essential for bringing the birds to breeding condition. At the Bear River Migratory Refuge whistling swans feed almost exclusively on sago pondweed.

On the other hand, whistlers that winter on the East Coast, particularly in the Chesapeake Bay region, supplement their vegetable diet with thin-shelled long clams and Baltic macomas. Fishermen of the area claim that the birds are destroying the commercial clam beds.

Criticism of swans, especially whistlers, has also come from duck hunters, who contend that because of their habit of treading holes in the mud and rooting up excessive amounts of various water plants, swans waste large quantities of valuable duck foods. Others believe just the opposite: that the swan's waste actually helps ducks by providing the smaller birds with food material which they might not have been able to reach otherwise. The annual return to the Bear River Refuge by hundreds of waterfowl, including many swans, does not indicate that swans damage the plant life. Whenever I have seen them feeding on underwater plants, there has been a retinue of ducks and coots in attendance, and each time a swan brought up a billful, the smaller birds dashed in for the scraps.

In addition to waterweeds, mute swans eat some small invertebrates, frogs and fishes. Bewick's swans consume land plants as well as aquatic

A trumpeter holds its head in this position when swallowing water.

ones, and during the flightless period when they frequent open stretches of water for protection, small fishes become a part of their diet.

The quantities of food required by swans varies according to many factors such as size of bird, temperature and energy demands. The food supplied to a flock of 17 captive birds at Red Rock Lakes may provide

an indication of how much is needed. It was July. The weather was mild. The birds were all young (nonbreeders) and probably averaged around 20 pounds each. Fifteen gallons of aquatic plants and 30 pounds of grain were fed each day—almost a gallon of plants and 2 pounds of grain for each bird. The gallon of vegetation, however, was a rather loose "water and weed" gallon.

Swans drink water in much the same way as do other fowl. Water is taken into the mouth by submerging the bill and is swallowed by elevating the head and neck. The bulge of water can be seen going down the swan's long neck.

A patient researcher once picked all the feathers from a whistling swan and counted them. There were 25,216 altogether; of these, 20,000 were small feathers from the head and neck. The whistling swan replaces these feathers each year. Fortunately, all are not shed at once. Along with the ducks and geese, however, swans do lose all their flight feathers at the same time and are unable to fly for about a month during the summer. There is undoubtedly some variation in the time of molting in different areas. Whistling swans, for example, molt somewhat later than trumpeters.

The trumpeters at Red Rock Lakes generally molt their flight feathers in July, but some may lose them as early as June, some not until August, September or October. Nonbreeders molt more or less at the same time, whereas for breeders molting extends over a longer period. The female swan usually loses her flight feathers first, about the time the eggs hatch, and as a result must stay on the water with her cygnets for a month or so. The male becomes flightless about the time the female becomes airborne again. This variation in molting schedule would appear to have some survival value, since at any given time at least one of a pair is able to get away from danger by flying. Also one

The neck of a trumpeter, if it is like that of the whistler, may have as many as 20,000 small feathers on it.

81

or the other of the parents has the power of flight during the entire brooding period. Both sexes of the Bewick's swan are reported to molt simultaneously.

Before losing their flight feathers black swans, and possibly other species, move to large open waters in what are called molt migrations. Such movements are limited to birds without cygnets, of course. During the flightless period they are vulnerable to danger and are unable to move far in search of food; consequently, they look for a safe place with abundant food.

In the summer of 1969 I had an opportunity to observe an unusual facet of trumpeter reaction. I had been invited to go along with refuge personnel in an airboat while they banded trumpeters at Red Rock Lakes. The procedure was to follow flightless birds with the boat; then when it overtook them one man controlled the boat while another captured the swans. While we were still a long distance away, the swans started swimming rapidly away from us. As we got close, they flapped their denuded wings and floundered across the surface, trying

During the molting period a flightless trumpeter tries to escape from a U.S. Fish and Wildlife capture boat. Note the plastic collar placed around its neck for research purposes.

vainly to get into the air. Sometimes a bird would dive as the boat overtook it. We then circled and tried again. Eventually, the bird tired and could be caught.

My odd discovery was that as soon as we touched a bird it became quite docile and could be lifted into the boat without frantic wing flapping. While we positioned the plastic collar around its neck, it lay quietly in the bottom of the boat. However, as soon as it was returned to the water, it immediately went back into its wing-flapping, foot-paddling escape routine. Apparently the touch of human hands had calmed the birds.

Again when I visited the Red Rock Lakes Refuge, personnel had been capturing birds for transplanting to other areas and now had 17 swans, all immature but with white adult plumage. They were being held in an enclosure, about 40 by 50 feet, which contained a pool some 20 feet in diameter. The birds had been overtaken and captured by the refuge airboat and by this time had been in the pen about a week. Such an experience should have made the birds nervous and excitable. Consequently, when I entered the enclosure, a stranger to them, I expected them to retreat to the far fence corner with loud trumpeting and wing flapping. I moved slowly to lessen the shock of my presence.

The swans faced me as soon as I opened the gate. They appeared to be interested but not alarmed; at least there was no panic. I worked my way slowly toward them. Finally, by the time I was within 10 feet of some and 15 feet of all, the birds had so accepted me that they probably would not have been upset by anything (short of attacking them) I could do.

I still have no satisfactory explanation for the conduct of these wild birds. Possibly trumpeters have an instinctive awareness of the futility of trying to escape when escape is not possible.

I have never been fortunate enough to be near a wild swan when it decided to take a bath, but I doubt that its actions would be very different from those of one old male mute swan that performed so

A mute swan takes a bath with seeming enjoyment and lots of splashing.

The long neck comes in handy.

With all the twisting maneuvers, it is a wonder that the neck ever gets straightened out.

The end of the bath.

beautifully for me on Mirror Pond in Bend, Oregon. Actually, it appeared to me that the swan bathed almost exactly as did the Canada geese and the ubiquitous mallards that shared the pond with it. Since the swan was much larger, the bathing was more spectacular and water splashed higher, but it involved the same head dipping, wing and foot thrashing and some roll overs—during which the big webbed feet waved in the air. While thrashing his wing, the bird would lean to one side or the other so that half the body was immersed. The bath ended with a beautiful neck and wing stretch.

An extended period of grooming and preening followed. Swans often spend so much time at this that it seems a matter more of vanity than of necessity. It is practically impossible, however, to overestimate the importance of feather care to swans, many of which nest in the cold Arctic wilderness and migrate thousands of miles twice a year.

According to one study involving the observation of captive trumpeters during a single 13-hour period, the birds preened on an average of five times and bathed once. In a similar study, trumpeters were

Below and opposite: A trumpeter swan preens.

timed during bathing and preening sessions, and it was discovered that most of them required from 21 to 40 minutes. However, one male, perhaps more vain, possibly dirtier than most, spent almost an hour and a half bathing and preening. Long preening periods were also observed for a captive black-necked swan (one and a half hours) and a captive whooper swan (one hour). Whether or not wild flocks would groom for such long periods is not known.

A Malheur Refuge trumpeter showed me how it could clean and preen itself without bathing first. This particular bird needed a bath. The feathers on its lower neck and chest were black with mud. Nevertheless, standing in shallow water (probably why it didn't bathe), it removed all dirt with its bill and head and then groomed its feathers.

The bird uses its bill and head feathers to collect oil from the preen gland (located at the base of the tail) and then to apply it to its plumage. Because it contains a large amount of fatty acid with some wax and fat, this oil conditions the feathers to retard drying and fraying, and keeps the surface of the bill healthy. The theory that oiling the feathers waterproofs the plumage now seems to have been partly disproved. Recent experiments have shown that the finely distributed air enclosed

in the barbules of the feathers is probably the main factor in water-proofing. The oiling, on the other hand, is apparently important in maintaining feather structure.

Although the daily routine of swans is undoubtedly variable, it does seem to follow a logical sequence, and paired birds perform more or less in unison. Several times daily the birds indulge in bathing, preening, sleeping, loafing, swimming and feeding. Captive trumpeters, like wild birds, did much of their preening, sleeping and loafing on land.

Little is known of swans' nighttime activities, but it seems reasonable to believe that they generally rest during darkness. On Mirror Pond in Bend, Oregon, though I've never noticed swans asleep at night, I have often seen ducks and geese—motionless silhouettes against the reflected wash of distant streetlights. Where the swans slept I have no idea, but I did not see them out feeding.

Captive trumpeter swans commonly spend the first hours of the day preening, then resting. Feeding increases around midmorning and reaches a peak in early afternoon. Next there is a lengthy rest period, another preening and then a feeding period in the late evening. Finally a period of extensive rest begins around dusk and appears to extend throughout the night.

Wild swans, however, may not follow the same schedule. The thousands of whistling swans that visit Bear River each fall seemed most active during the early morning.

For captive trumpeters, resting periods during the day lasted from a few minutes to an hour, sleeping periods from one or two minutes to 85 minutes. When sleeping, the trumpeter curves its long neck to the rear and rests the neck and head on its back. The tip of the bill (up to the nostrils) is normally tucked under a wing.

Trumpeters often indulge in shaking and stretching activities that are best described as "comfort" movements. There is a body shake that starts at the tail and moves forward, first to the wings, then on up the body and neck. This shaking, quite vigorous at times, fluffs the feathers and appears to rattle them all into position. Usually it follows a bird's exit from the water.

Sometimes the bird may shake the wings alone. The most spectacular of these shaking movements is a strong flapping of the wings. Although also done on land, this is most impressive on the water. First the swan paddles rapidly with its strong webbed feet, raising its body out of the water into a near-vertical position. Then it opens the wings and flaps them several times. Wing flapping occurs more or less regularly after bathing but may also be seen after an aggressive encounter or other disturbance.

Swans stretch wings and legs—sometimes together, sometimes separately—usually after an activity like preening or sleeping, during which muscles might become cramped. Probably, stretching loosens swans' muscles, just as it does for people.

A body shake usually follows a swan's exit from the water.

In a serene setting, a pair of trumpeter swans.

Autumn

SUMMER is a short season on the swan's northern breed grounds. Sometimes the race between a cygnet's growth and freeze-up is close. Sometimes the cygnet loses. If the fierce cold that comes early above the Arctic Circle catches young swans unable to fly or otherwise unfit for the long southward migration, they are doomed.

There is an apparent urgency in cygnets' feeding that may be an instinctive awareness of the necessity to eat great quantities so that their growth and development will be fast. Usually, there is little margin for laggards. Whistling swans hatch in late June and early July and require approximately 100 days to reach flight stage. This means that it will be late September at the earliest before the young swans are able to go south. And although the calendar says *autumn*, freezing temperatures are common by then.

Bewick's cygnets hatch in July, somewhat later than most whistlers, but seemingly develop much faster—cygnets have been reported able to fly 40 to 45 days after hatching.

Even though their nesting grounds are much farther south, some trumpeter cygnets at Red Rock are still flightless when freezing weather comes. Some can fly after only 91 days, while others take as long as 122 days.

For a month or so of this period, the nesting site is the swan family's loafing and preening place during the day and the cygnets' brooding spot at night. The nest gets mashed down, dirty with feces and so disrupted that at the end of the nesting season there is little, if any, resemblance to the original nest. Gradually, however, the old nest site ceases to be the center of family activity, and the swan family uses more of their total nesting territory. By autumn, territorial attachment is not strong. Broodless pairs may desert their home area completely.

The fact that the trumpeter stays on its nesting territory until autumn more or less prevents the combining of broods so common among Canada geese, though it does occur rarely. In August, 1955, aerial observers at Red Rock saw a single pair of trumpeters with 10 cygnets. Because of earlier nest checks in the area it could be determined that the abnormally large brood was due to the association of at least three normal broods. By August the cygnets would have weighed

Loafing around the nest site.

10 to 15 pounds and the parents would have relaxed their vigilance somewhat.

Nevertheless, family ties remain strong. Cygnets stay with the parent birds until the approach of the next breeding season. Families are readily distinguishable even in great flocks—they are small groups within a larger group. Brood mates remain together somewhat longer, it appears, at least until their first flightless molt (which comes during their second summer).

Trumpeter cygnets' first feathers appear at about six weeks, and thereafter seem to grow rapidly. In another 10 weeks or so the young birds have what is substantially a full complement of feathers and should be flying. At this age they are still immature, or juvenile birds,

The young whistling swan at left is almost as large as the whooper swimming next to it.

and though almost as large as the adults and able to travel with them, their plumage still has a distinctive color.

The juvenile trumpeter is brownish gray on the head, neck and upper back, and lighter gray underneath. The forehead, crown, occiput, nape and upper cheeks are light-reddish brown. The feet are yellowish or olive gray-black. The bill tends toward black, but the basal portion behind the nostril is salmon or light-pink color. In the rare white phase, the first feathers are white like those of the adults, but feet and bill are the same color as in the ordinary gray phase.

Immature whistlers are pale, warm gray on head, neck, back, sides and tail, and paler on breast and rump; below and on the underwing they are nearly white. The bill is flesh colored, with black on the edges and on the nail. The feet are flesh colored. Color varies in whistlers, probably with age, to the extent that some juveniles have feet and bills that are nearly black.

Both the whooper and Bewick's juveniles have substantially the same coloring as the whistler.

First-year mute swans are brownish with gray bills and feet. During their second year, when they are still immature, the feathers become white, the bill a dull orange; at this time the black forehead knob is present but small.

The young black swan's color is much the same as the young mute's. The black bill turns red when the bird is about five months old. The feet are dull gray. In the second year and after the first molt, juveniles look like the adult birds but are somewhat lighter.

The black-necked swan takes on a mixture of colors during its juvenile period. The white body feathers have rusty-gray tips on the upper parts and sides. The ends of the primaries are spotted with blackish gray. The neck is brownish black with gray flecks. The frontal caruncle is absent for the first year, although the bill is dull red at the base. During the second year the immature bird takes on most of its adult coloring, but the front caruncle remains small until the third (sometimes the fourth) year, when the bird becomes fully adult.

Even though most opinions on the senses of swans are based on observed reactions only, there is little doubt that sight and hearing are well developed. In November, 1970, I visited the Bear River Migratory Bird Refuge. At the time an estimated 15,000 or more whistling swans were there, most of them resting in several large impoundments bordered by dike roads. As I drove over some of these dike roads, I found that the swans feeding or resting near the road were always moving away by the time I saw them—even through binoculars, I could not locate any that seemed unaware of my approach. Most of them swam out until they were 400 or 500 yards from the dike. A few, less timid than the rest, would resume feeding when they had put only 100 to 150 yards of water between themselves and me.

The birds seem to take less extreme caution when they are in the air. Frequently, at Bear River, swans that kept 400 to 500 yards of water between my car and themselves would take off and fly right over it, no more than 150 feet in the air.

Trumpeters on the Malheur Refuge swam within 50 feet of a blind

Apparently accustomed to metallic sounds, the Malheur trumpeters were not alarmed at the sound of my camera shutter.

from which I was taking pictures, and did not seem concerned with the sound of my rather noisy motor-driven camera shutter. But their lack of fear was due, I think, to the location of the pond rather than to any hearing deficiency. The small body of water where the blind is located is near the refuge headquarters complex, from which comes a constant flow of metallic nonwild noises. The birds were simply accustomed to such things.

One morning I overslept and by the time I arrived at the pond it was fairly light. As soon as I came within view, a pair of swans that had spent the night began preparing to escape. I opened the gate in the fence that surrounds the pond and stepped inside. When I was still 100 yards away, the two birds became agitated, and as soon as I walked a couple of steps toward them they left. Going *inside* the fence seemed to be the nonroutine action that frightened the birds.

The trumpeter apparently has a remarkable ability to remember visual experiences and to govern its actions accordingly. In his monograph *The Trumpeter Swan,* Winston E. Banko described what happened one day when he departed from his observation post, a small shed near the water's edge. Usually he had had someone approach the lake from a distance, thus frightening away the swans; then, when the birds were gone, he left the blind. On this occasion, however, he stepped out in full view of a hundred or more swans. Almost immediately they took flight. Afterwards the swans apparently remembered the frightening incident; for the next four years they avoided moving close to the building.

A similar incidence of swan memory was reported for some wild trumpeters wintering in British Columbia. These birds were being fed grain by a private citizen, and one member of the family had so charmed them that they would take grain from her hand. Later, some of the birds were lured into a trap by use of grain, and for several years after, the birds would not accept hand-offered grain.

All swans are strong fliers, but because of their size they do not easily become airborne. Black swans, for example, require 40 to 50 yards for normal takeoffs, and in thick vegetation, among timber or in rough water, they cannot rise at all. In open water they are sometimes driven downwind by powerboats, and since they cannot rise from the water under such circumstances, they are caught. Once in the air their flight is strong but slow and graceful. They fly in long skeins or *V*'s. They may make flights around their home water during the day, but longer flights are usually made at night.

I once photographed a pair of trumpeters taking off from the display pond in the Malheur National Wildlife Refuge—probably a typical demonstration of trumpeters getting into the air. I was on a slight rise overlooking the pond, some 50 to 75 yards from the birds. My photographic equipment was a motor-driven Nikon F 35mm single lens reflex camera equipped with a 300mm Nikkor telephoto lens.

As soon as the two swans saw me they came to attention and began swimming toward the south end of the pond to my left. I was surprised; I had anticipated they would move directly away from me in what at first glance was a more logical line of retreat. Then I realized that they were getting into position for a takeoff and so had moved to that part of the pond that would give them the longest "runway."

Now ready to leave, the birds became more agitated and gave single, short, trumpetlike warning notes. Then, a half-wingbeat apart, they started off, their great wings thrashing the air, their large webbed feet pushing at the water with such force that it raised a splash a foot high. Since I was a fraction of a second late starting the camera, my sequence does not show whether or not the wing tips touched the water on their first powerful sweep. However, in subsequent wing action, the wing tips did not touch the water.

After making these pictures, I tested the sequential timing of the camera. I made from 25 to 28 exposures in 10 seconds. Using these figures and measuring the distance traveled between frames in terms of trumpeter body lengths (a length being assumed to equal 5 feet), I

From left to right across pages 98 and 99: A sequence showing a trumpeter's takeoff.

discovered some interesting probabilities. For example, the fact that the swans' wings are up in one frame and down in the following frame indicates that there are either approximately 12 to 14 wingbeats in 10 seconds or (and this seems more likely) double that number—24 to 28 beats in 10 seconds, or 2.4 to 2.8 beats per second. This latter figure substantially agrees with Richard Meinertzhagen's timing of the wing-beats of mute swans; he found that under several different flight conditions these varied from 2.6 to 3.2 beats per second.

There are 10 photographs in the sequence before the birds finally become airborne. This represents a four- to five-second takeoff time. Between the first and tenth photographs the birds covered approximately 100 to 110 feet, a measurement that agrees with other estimates of the length of run trumpeters require to build up sufficient speed to get them into the air. There was no wind on this particular

morning. If the swans are able to head into a wind, the takeoff distance is shortened.

The exertion needed for takeoff causes the long necks to undulate slightly with each wingbeat. But once the birds reach cruising speed they hold the necks motionless and point them straight ahead. As soon as the swan is airborne it pulls the feet and legs up and back under the body for streamlining. With the legs in this position the toes almost reach to the tip of the tail.

Trumpeters gain altitude rather slowly, and on purely local flights they stay low and travel a fairly direct route to their destination. Over flat terrain like marsh or water they often seem to go no higher than is necessary to keep their wings out of the water or ground cover. In familiar country they are creatures of habit, usually following the same routes from one place to another. If some unfamiliar obstacle has been

A mute swan in flight.

raised in their path, they may fly into it and injure or kill themselves because of their inability to maneuver quickly. Recent studies of Chesapeake Bay whistling swans indicate that, except when migrating, whistling swans rarely reach an altitude of 1,000 feet. Casual observations seem to confirm this for western-based whistlers as well. The 1,000-foot measurement, of course, represents altitude above ground level—which itself may be several thousand feet above sea level. When there are mountains in their path, the birds fly at the altitude required to get them over or around them.

When descending from great heights trumpeters sometimes cup their wings stiffly and come down in a steep, screaming approach much like

A trumpeter comes in for a landing.

the steep, fast descent of an aircraft using full flaps. More often than not, though, swans lose altitude slowly and gradually. As they near the water, their outstretched wings lower them slowly toward the surface, their feet drop and the webbed toes spread wide. Next, the tail sinks lower, the feet swing forward and the body becomes more vertical. As the widespread toes touch the water, the webs slide tobogganlike across the surface to slow the bird. Finally, the neck and head group and the wings start to fold, after which the swan quickly loses speed and is able to take its normal on-the-water position.

There have been some extravagant estimates of swan flying speed, but there is little evidence to support them. The cruising speed of Red Rock trumpeters was estimated to be 40 miles an hour, a figure arrived at by following the birds in a snowplane that nearly matched their speed. It is reasonable to assume that trumpeters in a hurry might go faster, possibly up to 50 to 55 miles an hour, a speed Charles S. Weiser reported for a flock of whistling swans. Weiser flew his light plane with and past the birds for several minutes. Since he based his figure on his own instrumented flight speed and the ease with which he overtook the flock, it seems a reasonable estimate.

The speed of Bewick's swan has been measured at 39 to 42 miles an hour, that of the mute swan at 31 to 40 miles an hour. The whooper has been clocked at 41 to 44 miles an hour.

With a strong tail wind pushing them swans will attain a much higher ground speed. Conceivably, therefore, if the aiding wind were strong enough, they could reach the unusually high ground speeds of 80 to 100 miles an hour that have sometimes been attributed to them.

The maximum altitude at which swans fly or have flown is not known, but whistlers have been seen at 8,000 feet. In fact, some years ago an airliner ran into some at that altitude. Trumpeters would have to fly higher than 7,000 feet to clear the mountains (the Centennials) between their summer home at Red Rock Lakes and their wintering

A pair of trumpeters in flight.

grounds in Idaho.

Flight formations vary greatly. Red Rock trumpeters may form irregular staggered formations or an offset line, or they may fly more or less abreast. On the Malheur Refuge, where I have never seen more than two trumpeters flying together, the pairs fly with one bird slightly behind and to the side (though I could not tell whether the lead bird was the male or the female).

103

Whistling swans. Even on short flights they seem to adopt a formation.

Whistling swans around the Malheur and Bear River refuge make local flights alone or in pairs and small groups. In the small groups the number of birds varies greatly. Most, however, seem to contain six or seven and are probably families to which singles or pairs may attach themselves. For example, in some of my photographs of these flying groups, the individuals seem to be separable as follows: a flock of six that is really two families of three each; a flock of seven that is two families (one of three, one of four birds); a flock of eight—a family of six and two singles; and one flock of 12—actually two smaller flocks of seven and five that have joined forces.

Whistler flights are usually in formation: sometimes a V (often a bit ragged), sometimes just a staggered line. If a large number of birds is involved, they may fly in a long curving line. On migration flights these swans have been reported flying both in V-shaped formations and in single lines of as many as 500 birds. Other migrating swans undoubtedly follow much the same procedure.

Flying in formation is not done simply to keep in touch with the rest of the flock. Actually it conserves the energy of all but the lead bird, and since swans change leaders from time to time, the formation helps them all. In flight, some air spills over the wing tips and results in a loss of "lift." At the same time this air spill creates an enlarging spiral vortex of air behind each wing tip and an upswelling of air on the outer side of each wing. In formation flying, birds follow one another behind and slightly to one side in order to rest their inner wing tips on the rising vortex from the wing of the bird in front. This provides extra lift for the following bird, which thus salvages some of the energy lost by the bird ahead.

In flight, the wings of all white swans except the mute are comparatively silent. The mute's wings produce a melodious, deep throbbing note, and a flight of several birds yields a strangely pleasant music. John K. Terres, in his book on bird flight, *Flashing Wings,* states that he could exactly imitate this sound by whispering "w-a-h! w-a-h! w-a-h!" steadily in the same rhythm as the wing strokes.

When flying, the black swan makes a similar sound with its wings, but this is a softer hum with a less musical whistle.

Earlier there was a mention of the different sounds made by the various swan species—from the loud hornlike trumpetings of the trumpeter to the subdued noises of the comparatively silent mute swan. The principal reason for the variation in sound-producing capabilities by the different species seems to be the length of the trachea (windpipe) and its position in the body cavity.

In man the vocal cords are in the larynx, at the upper end of the windpipe. In a bird, however, the vocal organ or *syrinx* is located at the lower end of the windpipe where it forks into two bronchi—each of which leads directly to the bird's lungs. Consequently, the fullness and quality of a bird's voice is thought to be affected by the length and shape of the windpipe it passes through.* Similarly, in brass musical instruments the pitch is determined not only by the shape and

Editor's Note: There are some recent doubts about this, and more research seems to be required before it is fully understood. See especially the statements of Greenewalt whose publication (1968) is listed in the Bibliography at the end of this book.

kind of mouthpiece used but also by the size, length and shape of the brass tubing through which the sound passes.

The northern swans—trumpeter, whistler, whooper and Bewick's —all have long and convoluted windpipes. That is, the windpipe extends inside and almost to the rear of the sternum (breastbone), then makes a reverse turn and comes out again. In the trumpeter, whooper and whistler, the windpipe may be more than 4 feet long. The mute, black and black-necked swans have relatively simple and unconvoluted tracheae.

The windpipe of the trumpeter also makes a vertical loop inside the sternum, although that of the whistling and Bewick's swan does not. Also, the trumpeter's trachea emerges through a separate opening in the sternum, whereas the whistler's both enters and exits the sternum at the same opening. It is thought that the extra loop in the trumpeter's windpipe accounts for much of the variation between the adult calls of the two American species.

The development of the windpipe within the sternum is progressive with age. In four- or five-month-old cygnets the windpipe barely enters the breastbone.

The trachea of the whooper also has a small upward loop inside the sternum, but this loop is a somewhat different shape from the trumpeter's.

Previously, I spoke briefly of the migratory habits of the different swan species. But the seasonal journeys of our whistling swan deserve additional attention, if for no other reason than that these birds are closer to home.

I always think of the spring migration to northern nesting grounds as a *return*, a *going home* journey, if you will. One reason might be that the nest is generally considered as the swan's home country. But to say this does not really answer the question of whether the swan started out in the north or in the south, which in turn brings up the problem of why birds migrate in the first place. And there are other mysteries of migration: how does a bird know when to migrate? and where? and how does it know how to get there?

These questions, which have intrigued scientists for years, have resulted in many theories, endless studies and millions of words of comment. We have learned, through birdbanding, where many species go, when they go and what routes they travel. Most of the rest is still subject to theorizing. For present purposes we must be content with the where and when and must leave the mysteries alone. It is enough for now to accept migration as a fact.

Each spring and fall I frequently hear the faint gabble of migrating geese and, if the skies are bright, am usually able to locate the distant threadlike formations by squinting, though sometimes when the clouds are low and threatening, I can only hear them. Strangely enough, and much to my regret, I have never seen a formation of migrating swans. Of course, I've seen airborne swans in formation but not high-flying birds headed for distant points.

Lloyd F. Gunther is manager of the Bear River Migratory Bird Refuge in northern Utah. Twice each year, in November and March, this is the gathering place for the largest concentrations of whistling

Migrating whistlers. Note the snow-covered hills in the background.

swans in the West. Nevertheless, Mr. Gunther informed me that during the day neither he nor any of his staff had ever observed what appeared to be migrating swans. It is their belief, he stated, that incoming flocks from the north arrive at night and can frequently be heard arriving. Some apparently come in over the surrounding mountains at an altitude of at least 7,000 feet. One of the refuge biologists reported seeing a flock at night, flying no more than 25 feet above the highway.

Migrating whistlers have been seen moving across northwestern Pennsylvania in daylight as well as at night. During the peak of their 1952 southern migration through this area, one observer—within 15 minutes—counted 50 flocks averaging 100 swans to the flock.

Around the middle of September, whistling swans begin to leave their Arctic nesting grounds, but they seem to go with reluctance and progress southward at a leisurely pace. Migration routes are not clearly defined. It appears, however, that most of the breeding population from western Alaska moves down the Pacific coast (with some rest stops along the way) to their wintering grounds around the Sacramento-San Joaquin Delta in California. Some whistlers from northern Alaska apparently move eastward across the Rocky Mountains and join the Canadian population as it moves south through the interior of Canada, then into northeastern Alberta. Lake Claire and Richardson Lake in Alberta are staging areas. Here concentrations begin to build around October 1, and aerial surveys have counted as many as 25,000 swans in the area.

From this point the populations separate and follow patterns set by ancient ancestors. Atlantic-bound birds head southeasterly over the prairies of Canada. They sweep eastward through North Dakota, Minnesota, Wisconsin and Michigan, occasionally resting in such places as Lake Erie and the Niagara River and finally reaching their wintering grounds on the Atlantic coast.

Western groups head southwestward. They make their rest stops in southern Alberta, drop down through Montana and Wyoming and then turn westward toward the Bear River delta in northern Utah, or Tule Lake in northern California. The first whistling swans usually arrive at Bear River during the second week of October, and populations peak in mid-November. Since 1960 the fall concentrations have exceeded 20,000 birds. In 1969 they were in excess of 41,000, a remarkable increase over the 1968 fall visitation of approximately 27,000 birds.

If the weather is not too severe, some swans spend the winter on the waterfowl refuges in northern Utah; however, most of them continue on to the more benevolent climate of the central California valleys.

Whistling swans usually arrive at Tule Lake in late October. These birds seem reluctant to move and will usually remain until freezing weather closes the waterways and drives them south. They have been seen at Tule Lake as late as December 11, almost a month after freeze-up.

There are records of arrivals in California's Sacramento Valley as early as November 3, but most birds do not reach the area until late November and early December. Whistling swans are the latest of all our waterfowl at their wintering grounds and are among the earliest to return north in the spring.

Over most of its range the migrating whistler has little to fear except from natural enemies. Swan hunting has been outlawed for a long time, though in recent years a limited amount of hunting has been authorized for specific areas of the western winter habitat.

The Migratory Bird Treaty Act of 1918 gave effect to the Convention Between the United States and Great Britain for the Protection of Migratory Birds in the United States and Canada, signed in 1916. The treaty closed the season on both our native swan species for a period of 10 years. Thereafter, swan hunting was to be subject to Federal regulation.

Since the passage of the Migratory Bird Treaty Act, many whistlers and trumpeters have been illegally killed by hunters who claim to

The snow goose has distinctive black wingtips; adult northern swans are completely white.

have confused them with snow geese. From my own field experiences with both swans and snow geese, I would say that anyone who confuses the two species at shotgun range is either too blind or too stupid to be allowed to handle a lethal weapon.

In 1956, a limited whistling swan hunting season in the Pacific flyway was proposed, but one was not authorized until 1962, in Utah. One thousand single bird permits were issued in 1962, and the same number each year after, through 1968. In 1969 the number was increased to 2,500 permits, and Nevada was allotted 500 permits. In 1970, Montana joined the states that permitted the hunting of whistling swans;

The trumpeter is four to six times larger than a snow goose. Its long neck and the absence of black wingtips make it readily distinguishable from the legal-to-kill snow goose.

its allotment was 500 permits, making a total of 3,500 whistling swan hunting permits for 1970.

That hunters have had less than spectacular success no doubt surprised those who expected the swans to be big easy targets. Only 41.5 percent (or less than half) of the Utah permitees killed swans in the seasons from 1962 to 1969.

I talked to a hunter who participated in one of the early hunts and he described the procedure as a form of pass shooting. Before dawn hunters positioned themselves along a dike separating the night resting

111

area from the feeding grounds. Later, when the birds flew over on their way to feed, the hunters whose hiding place chanced to be under the flight got shooting.

According to my informant, the size and speed of the swan is most deceptive.

I also inquired about the taste of swan and was told that his bird, which had been the focal point of a Thanksgiving dinner, was good and tasted like wild goose.

There have been and will be protests against swan hunting.* But so far, at least, the hunting in Utah appears to have had little, if any, effect on the swan populations. Midwinter whistling swan census figures for the Pacific flyway for 1960–1969 show:

1960	35,501
1961	40,784
1962	32,345
1963	46,327
1964	29,564
1965	42,646
1966	36,604
1967	48,926
1968	35,630
1969	74,879

Editor's Note: There are understandably strong objections to permitting the hunting of whistling swans in any state in which there are populations of the once almost extinct trumpeter swan still making its comeback. The danger is that most hunters could not distinguish a trumpeter swan from a whistling swan in the field. According to Banko and Mackay (1964), within the United States there are nesting groups of trumpeter swans in national wildlife refuges in Montana, Wyoming, Idaho, Nevada, South Dakota and Oregon. The total population of trumpeter swans in the United States, Canada and Alaska was estimated in 1966 to be no more than about 2,100 birds. Based upon its modest increase to these numbers from less than 100 birds in the early 1930's, the trumpeter swan was taken off the "rare" species list of the U.S. Fish and Wildlife Service in December 1968. Any threats to the remnant populations must be scrupulously avoided.

Autumn

In a letter dated December 28, 1970, Mr. Donald A. Smith, Assistant Director of the Utah Department of Natural Resources, Division of Fish & Game, states:

The Division believes expansion or reduction of current seasons should depend on the resource itself. If swan populations appear to be capable of withstanding greater pressure, and the sportsman interest remains high, we would feel justified in asking for an increase in the number of available permits. On the other hand, if problems with crippling loss, illegal kill, and poor hunter cooperation become apparent, a reduction in permits or even a complete closure may be indicated. Recommendations will be based primarily on the welfare of the resource. We strongly believe that decisions on future seasons should be based primarily on biological fact and not emotion or sentiment.

Swans have proven themselves to be desirable game birds in the field and on the table. Most hunters have the preconceived notion that bagging a swan will be a relatively simple matter. However, a few trips afield usually does a great deal to dispel this idea. The majority of the hunters who have had permits are enthusiastic about hunting swans. Additionally, the season provides more than 10,000 days of recreation to hunters in Utah. These are trips directed towards swans alone and are seldom combination hunts for swans and other forms of waterfowl. Any resource which provides recreation of this magnitude is both important and significant.

An immature whistler.

Trumpeters.

Winter

WINTER presents few hazards for swans capable of flight. They move south until they find suitable open water and food, and there, apparently, they stay until winter catches up with them, at which time they move on. The winter migration is thus a fairly leisurely journey.

It is not cold weather that forces swans to travel so much as it is the loss of food and water. I have no idea of how cold it would have to get before the swan's wonderful insulation of feathers and down would be ineffective, but the temperature would have to be extremely low. In the Yellowstone-Red Rock Lakes country, winter temperatures often drop to 30, 40, and even 50 degrees below zero, yet wintering trumpeters seem to get along fine.

If a stream is spring-fed, the moving water will often keep it from freezing, but during prolonged periods of extremely cold weather even these streams will freeze. Fortunately, in the Yellowstone-Red Rock Lakes area there are warm shallow waters that stay open all winter and provide food and shelter. These warm waters probably also offer swans some protection against extreme cold, but how important this is for survival as compared to the feed and water they provide, we do not know. During frigid periods swans are often seen out of the water loafing on the snow.

In sub-zero weather, trumpeters have been known to fly with their feet tucked up forward and concealed in warm feathers and down. No doubt the trumpeter uses the same procedure when it is resting on snow or ice and its feet get cold.

Food and open water are not the only requirements for trumpeters' wintering grounds. There must also be ample room for takeoffs and landings and sufficient level and open terrain to allow for good visibility and movement. Heavy adjacent cover is undesirable: this provides cover for predators and constitutes a hazard to birds in flight.

It seems fairly certain that the winter habitat provided by the warm springs in the Yellowstone-Red Rocks Lakes area is the principal reason that trumpeters did not become extinct within the contiguous United States. Because of these springs the small population of trumpeters breeding in the Red Rock Lakes area did not need to make long dangerous migrations into heavily hunted regions.

Winter

According to Winston E. Banko, the most important trumpeter wintering areas in this section are:

1. Island Park area, which includes Henry's Fork of the Snake River and its upper tributary waters (Idaho).
2. Red Rock Lakes Migratory Waterfowl Refuge (Montana).
3. Yellowstone National Park (Wyoming).
4. National Elk Refuge, Jackson Hole (Wyoming).
5. Madison River, and its tributary waters above the Meadow Lake Dam (Montana).

The Malheur Refuge, site of the first trumpeter transplants outside of the Yellowstone-Red Rock Lakes area, has proved to be a suitable year-round home for trumpeters. During the winter of 1970–1971, 25 trumpeters were counted on the refuge. Even though winters are cold and much of the water surface is frozen, the refuge has spring-fed ponds that remain open and can accommodate swans and other hardy resident species.

During the latter part of the winter, trumpeters in the Red Rock Lakes area congregate in fairly large flocks around open water. A few whistlers may spend the winter here, but they are much in the minority. It is primarily a trumpeter swan wintering ground.

Before the winter season has ended and while the breeding habitat at Red Rock Lakes is still a bleak frozen landscape, pairs and small groups of trumpeters loaf some 6 to 8 miles from the nearest open water. It is as if they wanted to be on hand early for first choice of nesting site. Whistling swans, which have a much greater distance to travel between wintering and breeding grounds, also show a tendency to start toward their breeding country before winter is over.

The effect of early winter on late-developing cygnets has been mentioned, but the deaths of grown trumpeters that are attributable to cold weather appear to be few. There is at least one report of ap-

117

parent winter starvation of trumpeters in the Jackson Hole area of Wyoming. In this particular situation the pair of trumpeters had eaten all the food in the small piece of open water available to them. One wonders why the birds did not fly to seek food elsewhere. Possibly, by the time their nourishment was gone they no longer had enough strength to become airborne. Similarly, when extremely low temperatures freeze wintering waters that are traditionally open, habit alone may cause the birds to stay and face starvation rather than move into another area where food is available.

Among trumpeters in British Columbia, Canada, starvation is apparently a significant factor during winters of abnormal cold. Here, also, despite sub-zero weather the swans stay on in their usual wintering grounds, and some starve or become so weakened that they can no longer take flight to escape coyotes or other predators.

Adult wild trumpeters are surprisingly free of disease. It is no doubt unwise to assume that all of them are 100 percent immune, but I have found no reports of diseased wild adults. Captive adults have died from avian tuberculosis, aspergillosis, pneumonia, silicosis, "dropsy," botulism, coccidiosis and various undetermined causes of diseases.

Cygnets at Red Rock have had deformed feet. In one case where the young birds could not stand, the deformity caused the death of all four cygnets, the total occupants in a single nest. It seems that no crippled cygnets survive, since no adults with deformed feet have been reported.

Like other wild animals, trumpeters and probably all other swans are hosts at one time or another to various parasites. Healthy birds normally have few; the weak or sick may have heavy infestation. Generally, parasites are not thought to be deadly by themselves, but if they occur in combination with other factors, they may cause death. Various kinds of internal parasites (flukes, tapeworms, roundworms, gizzard worms, and so on) have been found in swans. The most common external parasite is lice, but during the summer months leeches may attach themselves to the bird. These bloodsuckers infest most of the waters frequented by trumpeters in their southern ranges. For adults they are little more than a nuisance, but their effect on cygnets may be more serious.

Despite the hunting restrictions on both our native North American swan species, shooting and lead poisoning (an indirect result of shooting) are major causes of adult fatality. A 1957–1958 study of whistling swans in Utah's Great Salt Lake Valley showed that 50 percent of 58 dead swans examined had died as a result of gunshot and 17.2 percent from lead poisoning. Lead poisoning results when a bird ingests lead shot. In heavily hunted areas a great deal of spent lead shot comes to rest in the muddy bottoms of marshes and ponds. Swans and other waterfowl that dig into this mud for food pick up the shot. One swan examined in Utah contained 236 lead pellets. The digestive processes

Trumpeters have some external parasites, which may be why this one is scratching its neck.

of the swan transform part of the lead pellets into soluble lead salts. As a result, the gizzard becomes partially paralyzed and refuses to function, causing the bird to starve to death. Several whistling swans that died of lead poisoning had food impacted from the gizzard to the throat opening.

The loss of eight swans in an English zoo was a mystery until it was discovered that the zoo had been built on a marsh previously used by hunters of wild mallards. Spent shot still lay on the marshy bottom, where the swans picked it up.

In the Coeur d'Alene River area of northern Idaho, swans as well as geese and ducks have died apparently because of the zinc and copper carried in the river and deposited on vegetation.

On water or in the air, swans are graceful creatures with fluid movements which make them appear masters of their element. Yet, they are frequently involved in flying accidents.

Most accidents to swans are from flying into objects, chiefly power, telephone and fence wires. In Bend, Oregon, power and telephone wires, bridge abutments and so on have regularly taken a toll of young mute swans. The main body of the pond, which contains two right-angle bends, is between 400 and 500 yards in length, and 20 to 100 yards in width. Tall ponderosa pines guard one side of the pond, while houses, trees and a high playground fence line the other side. There is a footbridge 10 to 12 feet high across the center of the pond, and a street bridge with wires and such at both ends. Of the juvenile mute swans that learn to fly on the pond, some may see the obstructions soon enough to drop back into the water and avoid them. Others make frantic efforts to clear the bridges. Unfortunately, their young flight muscles are often not up to the task, and they crash into the concrete or wires—usually with fatal results.

A study made in England found that flying into wires and other obstacles was the predominate cause of death in mute swans. Some were killed by oil; a few were shot; others died of injuries (from fighting or from unknown sources); and a few were killed by becoming entangled in fishing tackle.

A whistling swan at the Bear River Refuge was found with its lower mandible torn away, the result, it was presumed, of becoming caught in a muskrat trap.

Occasionally, migrating whistlers that stop to rest on the Niagara River are swept over the famous falls to their death. One such accident is reported to have killed approximately 200 birds.

In the spring of 1954 northbound whistling swans flew into torrential rains and hail over Wisconsin. Officials of the Wisconsin Conservation Department who examined 35 dead swans stated that they must have been caught at a high altitude in a heavy hailstorm. The birds had broken necks, burst livers and hearts, lung hemorrhages and many bruises on their heads and bodies.

Young swans are most susceptible to predation during their preflight period, but even then the size and protectiveness of the parent birds appear to be effective deterrents. Observations on the nesting grounds of wild swans (except perhaps the trumpeter) are almost nonexistent, and there is little in the literature regarding cygnet losses due to predation.

Swan broods in the Yellowstone Park and Red Rock Lakes area suffer substantial losses—in some years as high as 50 percent—of cygnets in the preflight stage. Unfortunately, the causes of these losses are unknown. Diseases, accidents, weather and predators—all undoubtedly take their toll, but we do not know how many deaths are attributable to each factor.

On one occasion a large gull was seen to kill one cygnet and wound another when the parent birds moved away, frightened by the observer's boat. Without the distraction, the adult birds probably would have protected the cygnets. An otter was blamed for the deaths of all or part of a brood of five cygnets hatched in a Yellowstone Park lake. The otter was not seen attacking the young birds, but an examination

Mink may take an occasional cygnet.

of otter droppings around the lake disclosed fragments of cygnet down, bones, legs and foot skin.*

Several mute swan cygnets from the Mirror Pond flock in Bend, Oregon, were killed one summer by a marauding mink. Here again, no one observed actual kills, but a mink had been seen near the swans, and other evidence indicated it to be the guilty party. The cygnets

*The food habits and behavior of others are detailed in *The World of the Otter* by Ed Park, another Living World Book.—*The Editor.*

were about two months old at the time and probably weighted 3 to 5 pounds each.

After trumpeters learn to fly, predation does not appear to be a significant mortality factor. There are always some swans lost to predators, of course, and where conditions are favorable to the predators or where the swans are at a disadvantage these losses may be large.

Except in British Columbia, the coyote is not generally considered a threat to swan populations.

The Arctic wolf apparently does little damage to swan flocks.

Eleven wing-clipped cygnets being held in captivity were lost to predators, mostly great horned owls, with some raccoons.

In British Columbia, coyotes were considered the principal predator; horned owls preying on juvenile birds ranked second; the golden eagle, third.

A Montana observer saw two eagles attacking a swan at an estimated 1,000-foot altitude. The eagles alternated in striking the larger swan until they brought it to the ground, where they dispatched it in a matter of minutes. But spectacular as this conflict might have been, there is little evidence that either golden or bald eagles constitute a threat to the swan population—as a matter of fact, none of the natural predators seems to be a real menace.

Bewick's swan has no real enemies except humans. Arctic foxes apparently fear the adult birds and will run away when they see one.

Not much is known about the longevity of swans in the wild, but it is probably safe to assume that on the average their lives are shorter than those of birds having the safeguards of captivity. This is not true of all animals. Two that immediately come to mind are the pronghorn and the moose, neither of which take kindly to captivity (although the reasons why they do not are somewhat vague). But swans have been quite adaptable and have established some remarkable longevity records.

The mute swan has been reported to reach ages of 50 and 70 years. Captive trumpeters have lived for 29 and 32½ years. This last figure seems to be the current record. Whistling swan ages of 8, 9, and 19 years are reported, and a pair of black-necked swans in England had cygnets every year for 20 years, which would put their age at 23-plus years.

I have been unable to locate age records of other swan species, but no doubt they would be comparable.

Birds that share trumpeter breeding areas: the coot (above), the avocet (below), and, on the opposite page, the killdeer (top), and the sandhill crane (bottom).

Often seen in swan country are pelicans (above) and, on the opposite page, Canada geese (top) and snow geese (bottom).

This close-up view of a preening trumpeter shows the velvety quality of the magnificent plumage.

Man and the Swan

To THE PRIMITIVE PEOPLES of the world the swan was, first, a source of food. Later, its great size, majestic manners and graceful movements prompted its incorporation into man's growing awareness of spiritual values, which could be represented by the swan. The great white bird became an important symbol in the myths and religious ceremonies of many early cultures. Swan symbolism was most common among races of man in northern Eurasia, but it also occurred among the peo-

To early man, the swan was a symbol of power, grace, and beauty.

ples in the Mediterranean region, the terminal point for the winter migrations of some northern-breeding swans. Our own native Indians also used it in their ceremonies.

From this early acceptance of the swan as more than merely edible meat, there came an extensive mythology, followed by fairy tales, customs and traditions. Thus, too, the swan and its attributes, both real and imagined, have been the basis for literature, drama, arts and musical expressions.

There are many legends involving swans. One that has many variations concerns "swan maidens."

In Nordic mythology, swan maidens and Valkyries were sometimes one and the same. Valkyries were helmeted goddesses, grasping spears crowned with flame, their mounts the flying steeds that scattered dew in the valleys and hail on the forests from their manes. The destiny of warriors was in the Valkyries' power, and it was they who chose the ones who were to die in battle.

Some stories, in which their activities were not connected with war, told how they could turn themselves into swan maidens, or maidens in swan plumage. There were also some swan maidens who were not Valkyries.

According to the legend these strange and gracious creatures were especially fond of the lakes and pools of lonely forests. Here, when they wished, they removed their feathered cloaks, or swan shifts, and appeared as young, beautiful and desirable women. If a man happened upon a swan maiden without her feathers and was quick and skillful enough to steal the robe, the maiden would not be able to escape and would have to obey him.

An Icelandic legend tells of the ardent and faithful love between a man named Helgi and the Valkyrie Kara. Presumably, he had caught her without her cloak. According to the story, she accompanied Helgi to war dressed in her swan plumage. During battle she would fly above the fighting and sing a song of such charm and sweetness that

Man and the Swan

Helgi's enemies lost the desire to defend themselves. But then, one fateful day, while Kara hovered above Helgi, he struck at an adversary with great force, and his raised sword struck and fatally wounded his beloved.

Cygnus, or cycnus, the swan, is a central figure in several Greek legends. In one version, Cycnus, a son of Poseidon and Calyce, was

The swan can be a formidable adversary.

133

abandoned at birth by his mother and was raised by a swan. When Cycnus grew up he became an ally of the Trojans and was invulnerable. Achilles could not kill him with the customary weapons, so he smothered him with a helmet strap. Later, when he returned to cut off Cycnus' arms, Achilles discovered his fallen enemy had been changed into a swan.

In another version, Cycnus was a son of Apollo and Thyria. When a companion abandoned him, Cycnus became so distraught that he attempted to end his life by jumping into Lake Canopus; after his mother, Thyria, had jumped in also, Apollo changed them both into swans.

Zeus, chief of the Olympian gods, fell in love with Leda, wife of Tyndareus. While Leda was bathing in a pool, Zeus took the form of a dazzling white swan and seduced her; as a result Leda bore two children by the god.

A painting by Leonardo da Vinci entitled *Leda and the Swan* shows the nude Leda caressing the great white swan that is Zeus. At her feet the god's children are hatching from a single egg.

Cygnus the Swan is the name given to a northern constellation in the Milky Way.

In the Old Testament books Leviticus and Deuteronomy, swans are included among the unclean fowl, that is, not suitable for human food.

An Australian legend (attributed to a tribe in Victoria) holds that once, during a flood, men who took refuge on a mountain were turned into black swans when the rising water reached their feet.

The ancients thought that the swan had great musical ability, which found its most perfect expression at the time of the bird's death. The term "Song of the Dying Swan" has been known and used for so long that its origin is obscure. Even today the term "swan song" is generally used to describe some final action. For example, the last act of a public official whose term has expired might be described as his "swan song."

Man and the Swan

In the Dialogues of Plato, written around 370 B.C., Socrates referred to the "Song of the Dying Swan." People still wonder if swans really sing when they are about to die. The only positive report I have is by Dr. D. G. Elliott, a "reliable observer and celebrated naturalist," and it dates back to 1898. He described how after he had shot a swan, it fixed its wings and glided toward the ground, during which he heard a completely unfamiliar song from the dying bird. "Most plaintive in character and musical in tone, it sounded at times like the soft running of the notes in an octave. . . ."

In recent years over 4,000 whistling swans have been legally killed in the United States, and as far as I know, there have been no reports of "dying" songs from any of them. An apparently acceptable explanation for the sounds Dr. Elliott reported was offered in *Natural History* magazine for June, 1951, by Dr. John T. Zimmer of the American Museum's Bird Department. A reader had asked, "Does a swan sing a 'swan song' when about to die?"

Dr. Zimmer replied that a mild passage of air, such as might be expelled by a dying bird, through a swan's long convoluted windpipe would produce a subnormal (softer) musical note. He also suggested that the trachea might have been punctured by shot, thus preventing a normal amount of air from reaching the syrinx or "voice box." Again, the syrinx might have been damaged.*

Swans are also the subject of several musical compositions. A famous Russian ballet still being performed is *Swan Lake* (*Le Lac des Cygnes*), which is danced to a score by Tchaikovsky. The *pas de deux* (dance for two) from Act Three of this ballet is frequently presented separately as the "Black Swan Pas de Deux." Other notable musical pieces are *Le Cygne,* by Camille Saint-Saens, and *Ein Schwan,* by Edvard Grieg.

---

*Dr. Albert Hochbaum, waterfowl expert at Delta, Ontario, gives full credence to the dying swan's song in his book, *The Travels and Traditions of Waterfowl.—The Editor.*

135

In literature most American children are familiar with Hans Christian Andersen's story of the Ugly Duckling, the tale of a cygnet that thought it was a duckling and was unhappy with its appearance until it grew into a beautiful swan. The term "ugly duckling" is often used in modern times to describe a drab young girl who blossoms into a beautiful woman.

Several swan-based words are in general use. A "swan dive" for example, is a graceful dive performed with arms outstretched and the back gracefully arched. A "swan-neck" might refer to any of several mechanical contrivances resembling in outline the neck of a swan; it is also given to a woman who has a long, slender, white neck.

For a long time there has been a cake flour carrying the name "Swans Down." I remember it as one of my mother's favorites. Obviously, the trademark is intended to imply that cakes in which this flour is used will be "light as swan's down."

Swans have been the inspiration for many place names, especially Swan Lake. Within a relatively small area in Minnesota there are four Swan Lakes and a Swan Lake Outlet. Iowa, Missouri and Oregon also have Swan Lakes, and I presume that other states do as well. In downtown Portland, Oregon, there is a "Swan Island" that was formerly the site of the Portland Municipal Airport. It is no longer an island and the airport outgrew this Willamette River island long ago, but the name remains.

Swans have also been a frequent subject in postage stamp designs. The mute swan has been used on the stamps of Denmark, Finland, the Netherlands, Rumania, the U.S.S.R. and Sweden. The whooper swan has been so honored in Denmark, Finland, Iceland, Norway and Sweden; the black swan in Australia, Rumania, Western Australia, and as a zoo issue in Cuba.

Bewick's swan appears on a North Korean stamp, and an unidentified swan illustration, apparently based upon the mute swan, appears on a Japanese stamp.

The black-necked swan is a central theme of several stamps of the Falkland Islands.

American swans are represented on two issues of United States waterfowl hunting permit stamps, the trumpeter in 1950 and the whistling swan in 1966.

Though there is uncertainty as to whether or not the mute swan originally occurred in England as a wild bird, opinions favor considering it a native. It has enjoyed the protection of the Crown and has been a Royal Bird to Englishmen for about 800 years.

When the Royal designation was first given to the mute swan it served to establish ownership of all the swans in the country, which by that time were mostly domesticated. After the ruling, people could keep swans on private waters; they also had the right to pursue and recapture any that escaped, as long as the pursuit was continuous. All other swans on open or common water belonged to the Crown. The Crown could, and did, grant to subjects the privilege of keeping swans on open and common waters, as long as the privately owned birds were pinioned and marked by the owner.

Swan marking is similar to the branding of livestock as practiced in the American West, but instead of the brands made with a hot iron, notches or lines are cut on the upper mandible of the young birds where they can be seen when the bird is on the water. Occasionally nicks or cuts are made on the webs of the toes or on the legs.

One seventeenth-century Englishman described his swan mark as follows: "Our mark is three holes boared with a hotte swipple in the right side of the nebbe (bille), and a gagge cut betwixt the uppermost holes, viz., that next the head and the other."

At one time, it is said, there were over 900 such marks in use. The Master of the King's (or Queen's) Swans (also called the Royal Swanherd) was responsible for registering all these brands and the supervision of the annual swan roundup.

This annual roundup is called "Swan-upping" and takes place when the cygnets are well grown but unable to fly. In the past, family groups were gathered and the young birds marked. Whenever the parent birds bore the marks of different owners, half the cygnets went to each. Also one young bird was usually allotted to the owner of the land where the birds had nested. Finally, there were local customs governing the disposal of the odd bird, should the brood contain uneven numbers.

Great prestige was attached to the keeping of swans: inasmuch as they were Royal Birds, simply to possess them gave the owner distinction. And, of course, because they could be given only by those permitted to keep such Royal Birds, the gift of a swan was rare and brought great honor to the donor.

Swans were also highly esteemed as food, and prior to the advent of the turkey they were the customary Christmas dish. Large banquets normally had one or more swans on the menu; occasionally they were served in great numbers. For his Installation Feast in 1466, George Neville, Archbishop of York, provided some 400 swans at his palace Cawood, near York.

Modern England no longer practices swan keeping to this extent; now most mute swans are feral—though descendants, probably, of these ancient domesticated birds. There is a remnant of the ancient swan-keeping rituals in the annual swan-upping on the Thames River. Here, two of the ancient but still-surviving London guilds, the Vintners and the Dyers (appropriately costumed—though not so lavishly as in former times) catch and mark swans for their Worshipful Companies and for the queen.

Swans were present on the North American continent long before the ancestors of the American Indian first crossed over from Asia on the Bering Sea land bridge. Fossil remains of swans, both trumpeters and whistlers, have been found in Pleistocene material in locations as widely separated as Oregon, Illinois and Florida.

The primitive Indians used swans principally for food, but undoubtedly the feathers were used for decoration and other purposes

A trumpeter swan "talking."

—while the body skin, with its covering of down and feathers, could have made warm robes or clothing. Often these people turned leg bones into implements and other bones into beads. Some early tribes believed that there was special magic in swan's down and in its wing bone.

In his book *Arctic Birds of Canada*, Lester L. Snyder describes an interesting use of swan feathers. Eskimos hunt seals by first locating in the snow the small aperture that marks the breathing hole of a seal in the ice below. Next, the hunter attaches a bit of swan's down to the snow in the tiny opening. Then he waits—silent and motionless. When the seal returns and rises to breathe, the upward surge of water is transmitted through the air and the sensitive down moves. The native then plunges his harpoon into the opening.

Swans were mentioned by the white settlers in this country as early as 1632. By the early 1700's they had recognized that there were two separate species, "the one we call trompeters because of a sort of Trompeting Noise they make." The writings of this period pointed out that the young cygnet was a desirable food and that the young birds were gray, not white like the older ones.

During the latter half of the eighteenth century swan skins became an article of commerce for the Hudson's Bay Company, and in the early part of the following century traders began dealing in swan skins in the lands that would later be Minnesota and South Dakota. Swan skins and feathers were used for decoration and swan's down for powder puffs, among other things. The quills made excellent pens. John James Audubon said he preferred trumpeter quills for fine detail because they were "so hard, and yet so elastic, that the best steel pen of the present day might have blushed, if it could, to be compared with them."

Many early records of swan observations are somewhat confusing since they make no distinction between whistling and trumpeter swans. However, it appears that the principal trumpeter breeding territories in the contiguous United States were the Red Rock Lakes, Yellowstone and Jackson Hole areas, the Flathead Valley of western Montana and the lands of southern Minnesota and northern Iowa. In addition, there were probably a few breeding birds in between these areas (where the terrain was suitable) and also east into Illinois and northwestern Indiana, but their number must have been small. The largest part of the original breeding grounds for trumpeters appears to have been north, in Canada and Alaska. However, there is no available evidence that trumpeter swans bred east of James Bay in eastern Canada.

From these breeding grounds trumpeters in the past migrated to wintering areas along the southeast coast of Alaska, on the west coast of British Columbia, Puget Sound, the lower Columbia River and in the central valleys and along the coast of California. They also wintered in the Red Rock Lakes-Yellowstone area, in the Mississippi and Ohio River valleys, along the Gulf coasts of Texas and Louisiana, in northeastern Mexico and on the estuaries of the central Atlantic states.

As the population of the United States increased and advanced westward, the trumpeter swan population diminished. In 1838, Audubon reported that it seemed to be gone completely from the eastern seaboard, although there were still trumpeters along the lower Ohio and Mississippi rivers. As late as 1890, migratory flocks of 75 to 1,000 trumpeters were seen in Texas, but by 1909 these too were gone.

Trumpeters were first reported from Alaska in 1850, but they seem to have been relatively unimportant to the early economy of the country, and the records are quite meager. Naturalists paid little attention to these Alaskan swans until after 1950. In 1957, about 200 trumpeters were discovered on the Kenai Peninsula. Subsequent wintering estimates and breeding ground surveys have indicated that there are at least a thousand trumpeters in Alaska and western Canada.

Both whistling and trumpeter swans were harvested during the fur-trading period. The trumpeter population appears to have suffered more, probably because its breeding territories were more accessible to the Indians of Canada who harvested eggs and flightless birds during the breeding season.

In 1932, a ground census was made of the trumpeter swans in the United States (exclusive of Alaska) in all areas known to have wild swan populations. Although, because of the nature of the country and the observation procedures then in use, the count was considered to be somewhat lower than the actual number of birds, the recorded total of 57 adult birds and 12 cygnets seems disastrously low. In fact, many concerned individuals believed that the trumpeter swan was doomed to follow the passenger pigeon and the heath hen into extinction.

In 1935, the Red Rock Lakes National Wildlife Refuge was established to protect the largest known remaining population of trumpeter swans. The count on the refuge that year showed 30 adults and 16 cygnets. Within 10 years there were 163 trumpeters on the refuge; by 1955, 283. In December, 1968, when the total of all trumpeter swan populations was estimated to be 5,000, the bird was removed from the U.S. Fish and Wildlife Service list of rare species.

At one time great numbers of whistlers wintered on the Gulf coast of Texas, but now these are all gone. Nevertheless, even though the whistling swan undoubtedly suffered at the hands of man, its losses did not reach the proportions of the trumpeter. Probably the reason for this is that the whistler was available primarily during fall and winter when its cautious nature and great flying ability gave it protection. When it is nesting, and so is more vulnerable, it lives so far north as to offer comparatively little opportunity for man's predation.

I have found no population figures for mutes, whoopers, Bewick's, black and black-necked swans; on the other hand I have found nothing suggesting that any of these species are in jeopardy, although most populations have been reduced, sometimes drastically, by man. In

Park visitors enjoy feeding the giant mute swans.

the past as many as 300 whoopers at a time were taken on the Russian breeding grounds by means of "swan drives" during the molt. Reduced populations have made this kind of hunting unprofitable in recent years; nevertheless, some hunting with nets continues in Iran.

All swan species have been kept and reared in captivity, and a substantial number of small populations are scattered throughout many different countries. This, in itself, would have some survival value if any of the wild populations were threatened.

The progress of the trumpeter population back from extinction is hopeful; perhaps it means that man has learned enough to ensure the continuation of all swan species.

Perhaps man has learned to ensure the continuation of all swan species.

Bibliography

Allen, Glover Morrill, *Birds and Their Attributes*. New York: Dover Publications, Inc., 1962.

American Ornithologists' Union, *Check-List of North American Birds*. Baltimore: American Ornithologists' Union, 1957.

Bailey, Alfred M., *Birds of Arctic Alaska*. Denver: The Colorado Museum of Natural History, 1948.

Banko, Winston E., *The Trumpeter Swan: Its History Habits and Population in the United States*. North American Fauna 63. Washington, D.C.: U.S. Government Printing Office, 1960.

————, and R. H. Mackay, "Our Native Swans," in *Waterfowl Tomorrow*. Washington, D.C.: U.S. Department of Interior, 1964.

Barrett, Charles, *Australian Bird Life*. Melbourne: Oxford University Press, 1945.

Barrett, Keith, "A Trumpeter Winter Resort," *Nature Magazine*, 49:34–35 (1956).

Batten, L. A., "Bewick's Swan," *Birds of the World*, 1:195–196 (1970).

Brock, Jeremy, "Whooper Swan," *Birds of the World*, 1:190–192 (1970).

Delacour, Jean, *The Waterfowl of the World*, Volume One. London: Country Life, Ltd., 1954.

————, and Ernest Mayr, "The Family Anatidae," *The Wilson Bulletin*, 57:3–55 (1945).

Dementiev, Georges P., and N. A. Gladkov, *Birds of the Soviet Union*, Volume IV. Washington, D.C.: U.S. Department of the Interior and the National Science Foundation, 1967.

De Vos, A., "Observations of the Behaviour of Captive Trumpeter Swans During the Breeding Season," *Ardea,* 52:166–189 (1964).

Eklund, Carl R., "Mortality Notes on the Trumpeter Swan," *Auk,* 63:89–90 (1946).

Featherstonhaugh, Duane, "Return of the Trumpeter," *Natural History,* 57:374–381 (1948).

Fisher, Arthur H., "Swans," *Nature Magazine,* 7:407–408 (1940).

Frith, Harold J., *Waterfowl in Australia.* Sydney: Angus & Robertson Pty., Ltd., 1967.

Gabrielson, Ira N., "Trumpeter Swan in Alaska," *Auk,* 63:102–103 (1946).

————, and Stanley G. Jewett, *Birds of Oregon.* Corvallis: Oregon State College, 1940.

Greenewalt, Crawford H., *Bird Song: Acoustics and Physiology.* Washington, D.C.: Smithsonian Institution Press, 1968.

Guerber, H. A., *Myths of Greece and Rome.* New York: American Book Company, 1893.

Hammer, Donald A., "Trumpeter Swan Carrying Young," *The Wilson Bulletin,* 82:324–325 (1970).

Harrison, C. J. O., "Mute Swan," *Birds of the World,* 1:186–190 (1970).

Hochbaum, H. Albert, *The Travels and Traditions of Waterfowl.* Minneapolis: The University of Minnesota Press, 1955.

Howard, William Johnston, "Notes on the Nesting of Captive Mute Swans," *The Wilson Bulletin,* 47:237–238 (1935).

Hudson, William H., *Birds of La Plata.* New York: E. P. Dutton & Co., 1920.

Innis, Pauline, "Wild Swans Risk Crash Landings for Corn," *Audubon,* 66:304–305 (1964).

Innis, Pauline B., *The Wild Swans Fly.* New York: David McKay Company, Inc., 1964.

Johnsgard, Paul A., *Handbook of Waterfowl Behavior.* Ithaca: Cornell University Press, 1965.

————, *Waterfowl: Their Biology and Natural History.* Lincoln: University of Nebraska Press, 1968.

Bibliography

Kortright, Francis H., *The Ducks, Geese and Swans of North America.* Harrisburg: The Stackpole Company, 1942.

Lack, David, "Pair Formation in Birds," *The Condor,* 42:269–286 (1940).

Leach, Maria, ed., *The Standard Dictionary of Folklore, Mythology, and Legend.* New York: Funk & Wagnalls Company, 1949.

Lint, Kenton C., "Cygnets from the South—Black-Necked Swans," *Modern Game Breeding,* Vol. 2, No. 10 (August, 1966), pp. 13–15, 40.

Mackay, R. H., "Movements of Trumpeter Swans Shown by Band Returns and Observations," *The Condor,* 59:339 (1957).

McKinney, F., "The Comfort Movements of Anatidae," *Behaviour,* 25:120–220 (1965).

Meinertzhagen, Richard, "The Speed and Altitude of Bird Flight," *Ibis,* 97:81–117 (1955).

Miers, K. H., and Murray Williams, "Nesting of the Black Swan at Lake Ellesmere, New Zealand," *Wildfowl No. 20,* Slimbridge, Gloucestershire, England, 1969.

Minton, C. D. T., "Pairing and Breeding of Mute Swans," *Wildfowl No. 19,* Slimbridge, Gloucestershire, England, 1968.

Moffitt, James, "Notes on the Distribution of Whistling Swan and Canada Goose in California," *The Condor,* 41:93–97 (1939).

Monnie, James B., "Reintroduction of the Trumpeter Swan to Its Former Prairie Breeding Range," *Journal of Wildlife Management,* 30:691–696 (1966).

Monson, Melvin A., "Nesting of Trumpeter Swan in the Lower Copper River Basin, Alaska," *The Condor,* 58:444–445 (1956).

New Larousse Encyclopedia of Mythology. New York: The Hamlyn Publishing Group Limited, 1968.

Ogilvie, M. A., "Population Changes and Mortality of Mute Swan in Britain," *Wildfowl No. 18,* Slimbridge, Gloucestershire, England, 1967.

Ogilvie, Malcolm, "Black Swan," *Birds of the World,* 1:184–186 (1970).

Paca, Lillian Grace, *The Royal Birds.* New York: St. Martin's Press, Inc., 1963.

Pakulak, Allan J., and Carrol D. Littlefield, "Breeding Status of Whistling Swans near Churchill, Manitoba," *The Wilson Bulletin,* 81: 464–465 (1969).

Perrins, C. M., and C. M. Reynolds, "A Preliminary Study of the Mute Swan, *Cygnus olor,*" *Wildfowl No. 18,* Slimbridge, Gloucestershire, England, 1967.

Peterson, Roger Tory, *The Birds.* New York: Time Inc. Book Division, 1963.

Phillips, John C., and Frederick C. Lincoln, *American Waterfowl.* Boston: Houghton Mifflin Company, 1930.

Schorger, A. W., "The Trumpeter Swan as a Breeding Bird in Minnesota, Wisconsin, Illinois, and Indiana," *The Wilson Bulletin,* 76:331–338 (1964).

Scott, Peter, "The Bewick's Swans at Slimbridge," *Wildfowl No. 17,* Slimbridge, Gloucestershire, England, 1966, pp. 20–26.

Sharp, Ward M., "Observations on Predator-Prey Relations Between Wild Ducks, Trumpeter Swans and Golden Eagles," *Journal of Wildlife Management,* 15:224–226 (1951).

Sharritt, Grace V., "Our Swans Trumpet Good News," *Nature Magazine,* 42:316–318, 340 (1949).

Sherwood, Glen Alan, "The Whistling Swan in the Great Salt Lake Valley of Utah." M.S. thesis, Utah State University, Logan, Utah, 1959.

Sherwood, Glen, "The Whistling Swan in the West with Particular Reference to Great Salt Lake Valley, Utah," *The Condor,* 62:370–377 (1960).

Simon, James R., "First Flight of Trumpeter Swans," *Auk,* 69:462 (1952).

Sladen, William J. L., "Studies of the Whistling Swan, 1967–68," *Transactions of the Thirty-Fourth North American Wildlife Conference.* Washington, D.C.: Wildlife Management Institute, 1969, pp. 42–50.

Snyder, Lester L., *Arctic Birds of Canada.* Toronto: University of Toronto Press, 1957.

Stefferud, Alfred, ed., *Birds in Our Lives.* Washington, D.C.: The United States Department of the Interior, 1966.

Bibliography

Stewart, Robert E., and Joseph H. Manning, "Distribution and Ecology of Whistling Swans in the Chesapeake Bay Region," *Auk,* 75:203–212 (1958).

Tate, James, Jr., and D. Jean Tate, "Additional Records of Whistling Swans Feeding in Dry Fields," *The Condor,* 68:398–399 (1966).

Terres, John K., *Flashing Wings.* New York: Doubleday & Company, Inc., 1968.

Thompson, Daniel Q., and Marjory D. Lyons, "Flock Size in a Spring Concentration of Whistling Swans," *The Wilson Bulletin,* 76:282–285 (1964).

Ticehurst, Norman F., *The Mute Swan in England.* London: Cleaver-Hume Press, Ltd., 1957.

Truslow, Frederick Kent, "Return of the Trumpeter," *National Geographic,* 118:134–150 (1960).

Van Tyne, Josselyn, and Andrew J. Berger, *Fundamentals of Ornithology.* New York: John Wiley & Son, Inc., 1959.

Weiser, Charles S., "Flying with a Flock of Swans," *Auk,* 50:92–93 (1933).

Wetmore, Alexander, "Remains of a Swan from the Miocene of Arizona," *The Condor,* 45:120 (1943).

————, "A Record of Trumpeter Swans from the Late Pleistocene of Illinois," *The Wilson Bulletin,* 47:237 (1935).

Zimmerman, John E., *Dictionary of Classical Mythology.* New York: Harper & Row, Publishers, Inc., 1964.

Index

Italic page numbers denote illustrations.

153

Index